OLYMPIC
BLACK WOMEN

OLYMPIC BLACK WOMEN

Martha Ward Plowden
Illustrated by
Ronald Jones

PELICAN PUBLISHING COMPANY
Gretna 1996

*The word "Pelican" and the depiction of a pelican are
trademarks of Pelican Publishing Company, Inc., and are
registered in the U.S. Patent and Trademark Office.*

Library of Congress Cataloging-in-Publication Data

Plowden, Martha Ward.
    Olympic Black women / Martha Ward Plowden ; illustrated by Ronald
Jones.
        p.   cm.
    Includes bibliographical references (p.   ).
    ISBN 1-56554-080-8 (alk. paper)
    1. Afro-American women athletes—Biography. 2. Olympics—History.
I. Title.
GV697.A1P56 1995
796'.092'2—dc20
[B]   95-32067
                                      CIP

Manufactured in the United States of America

Published by Pelican Publishing Company, Inc.
1101 Monroe Street, Gretna, Louisiana 70053

To my mother,
Mrs. Annie Mae Ward,
and to my daughter,
Natalie Ward Plowden.

And to the memory of my mother-in-law,
the late Mrs. Lucille M. Plowden,
and to my father-in-law,
the late Mr. George W. Plowden, Sr.

CONTENTS

Introduction 9

History of the Ancient Olympics 15

History of the Modern Olympics 19

    Evelyn Ashford 23

    Valerie Brisco-Hooks 29

    Earlene Brown 33

    Chandra Cheeseborough 39

    Alice Coachman 43

    Isabelle Daniel 47

    Gail Devers 53

    Mae Faggs 57

    Barbara Ferrell 63

    Benita Fitzgerald-Brown 67

    Zina Garrison 71

    Florence Griffith-Joyner 77

    Martha Hudson 83

    Barbara Jones 87

    Jackie Joyner-Kersee 91

    Mildred McDaniel 97

    Edith McGuire 101

    Madeline Manning 107

    Margaret Matthews 113

    Wilma Rudolph...119

Gwen Torrence 125
Wyomia Tyus 131
Martha Watson 137
Willye White 141
Lucinda Williams 147
Athletic Organizations 151
Black Women in the Olympics....................................159
Olympic Sites 163
Glossary 165
Further Suggested Reading 171

INTRODUCTION

Throughout history, women's participation in sports has always been an issue. The Ancient Greeks excluded women from the Olympic competition and even barred them from attending the games. Later, the women established their own Olympics, which was held one month before the regular Olympics and called the Heraean Games. Women in Sparta were encouraged at an early age to participate in sports activities, such as running, jumping, and javelin throwing, because it was felt that these sports would make them better breeders. There were others who felt that sports would build character, perseverance, strength, and respect for authority. Because these traits were considered irrelevant for women, there was not a need for their participation in sports.

Even Pierre de Coubertin, during his twenty-nine years as leader of the International Olympic Committee, found it impossible to encourage vigorous events for women in the Summer Olympic Games. He felt that women had but one task in the Olympics and that was to crown the winner with garlands. He felt that it was shocking to see women lightly clad and participating in strenuous activity. During the Dark Ages, it was felt that anything that was pleasurable was sinful and later, the feudal concept of chivalry did not permit women of the higher social classes to participate in anything of a physical nature. During the Victorian era, little was done to encourage women to participate in sports because it was felt that women should portray the desired image of gentility and helplessness. Yet, it was during this period that women's athletics became important: races were held at fairs and local festivals, in which women were allowed to participate.

Later, sports became a compulsory part of the education program in schools and races were organized for girls and boys.

During the first three decades of the twentieth century, society slowly forgot about the Victorian ideal of the frail woman and started involving women in physical activities. Women were first allowed to participate in the Olympics in 1900 at the II Olympiad, held in Paris, France. Eleven women and 1,066 men participated in this Olympics. Although women were allowed to participate in this Olympics, the American Olympic Committee restricted their participation to floor activities only. The female swimmers in 1920 were the first American women to receive full Olympic status.

Black women's participation in sports was kept separate from white women's until long after the abolition of slavery and the emancipation. It was during this time with emancipation and the procurement of land and material goods that many black women were able to participate in sports that required equipment and recreational facilities. Around 1890, there were some black families who owned tennis courts and around 1895, black colleges began organizing tennis matches and tournaments for their students.

African-Americans were still excluded from the white sporting organizations, so the American Tennis Association was organized in 1916. After World War I, community groups, such as churches, Young Women's Christian Association, public schools, and others, provided additional opportunities for African-Americans to participate in some sports. These sports included basketball, swimming, and tennis; and later there were track programs for women at some of the black colleges. Track for African-American women became very visible in the 1920s because of institutions like Tuskegee Institute, Tennessee State University, New York Mercury Club, Illinois Women's Athletic Club, and many others.

In the 1930s the New York Mercury Club provided a place for African-American women to train for track and field sports. Also in the thirties, the Unified Golfers Association was organized to assist African-American women golfers. In 1931, the Philadelphia Tribune girls' basketball team was organized, and they toured the country competing against both all white and all black teams. In 1937, Tuskegee track and field team set a precedent by winning the National AAU Championship and they remained undefeated until in the 1940s.

It was not until 1932 that the first African-American women were selected to participate in the Olympics in Los Angeles, California. They were Tydie Pickett and Louise Stokes. The year 1946 became a significant point in the development of African-Americans' participation in American athletics. Throughout history, African-American women had to fight for the right to enter national and international competition. Once given the opportunity, they competed and excelled in sports.

It was not until 1948 that African-American women achieved success in the Olympics. Tennessee State University and Tuskegee Institute had students who competed in the XIV Olympiad in London, England. They were Alice Coachman, in the high jump; Nell Jackson, in the 200-meter dash; Mabel Walker, in the 100-meter dash; Audrey Patterson, in the 200-meter dash; Emma Reed, in the broad jump; Therese Manuel, in the javelin and the 80-meter dash; Mae Faggs, in the 200-meter dash; Bernice Robinson, in the 60-meter dash; Lillian Young, in the 60-meter dash. The following women also participated on the U.S. Olympic team: Mae Faggs, Nell Jackson, Evelyn Lawler, and Jean Patton in the 400-meter relay. Alice Coachman won a gold medal in the high jump and Audrey Patterson won a bronze medal in the 200-meter dash.

In the 1950s the Indianapolis Clowns became responsible for African-American women's involvement in professional baseball. Between 1953 and 1956, Mildred McDaniel became the national AAU Champion (1953), the Pan American Games Champion (1955), and the Olympic Games Champion (1956) in the high jump.

More progress for African-American women was made in the Olympics between 1956 and 1972 when Dr. Dorothy Richey became the first African-American director for both men's and women's sports. During that time period, Nell Jackson became director of athletics twice, and both she and Willye White became members of the board of the U.S. Olympic Committee. And additional progress was made with the assistance of the

11

National Association for the Advancement of Colored People in 1954 with the *Brown v. Board of Education* and the passage of Title IX of the Civil Rights Act in 1972 and its implementation on July 21, 1975.

Presently African-American women are participating in all areas of track and field, tennis, basketball, rowing, volleyball, figure skating, and other sports. This book highlights some of the accomplishments of Olympic medalists in the sports arena.

OLYMPIC
BLACK WOMEN

HISTORY OF THE
ANCIENT OLYMPICS

The first historic Olympiad was held in 776 B.C. and took place every four years during the pre-Christian era. For many centuries the events were religious festivals and were observed only by those who lived in Greece. Gradually, the gatherings attracted more and more worshipers and the games and contests were added to the festivals.

There are many legends about the origin of the ancient Olympic Games: first, that it was founded by Hercules, the son of the god Zeus, to celebrate his great skills; second, that the two mighty Greek gods, Zeus and Cronus, were in a battle on the hills above the Olympia and the games and religious ceremonies were organized as a tribute to Zeus' victory. The third legend is that the games were a way of honoring Hercules.

Whichever legend was true, the Greeks chose to celebrate the games at the sacred valley of Olympia, which was located on the western coast of the Grecian peninsula near the Mediterranean Sea. The valley was surrounded by mountains with groves of pine and olive trees and through it ran the Alpheus River.

The main purpose of the athletic contests and the Olympic Games was the development of physical strength and skill. Initially, only men were allowed to participate and attend the events.

In the beginning, only one award was given because there was only one event and the first-place winner was the only person recognized at the ancient Olympics. The winner received an olive wreath (the symbol of victory) and the winner's, his father's, and his country's names were shouted out. The whole city celebrated the victory. Poems were written and lyrics were sung by youth choirs. The winner's deeds were chiseled on stone pillars and sculptors made life-size statues of him. The winner was exempted from paying taxes for life and given expensive presents, even sometimes money, depending on the wealth of the honored city.

The first Olympiad event was the Strade-race. The winner of the race was Coroebus of Elis, who was a cook. In 724 B.C. at the fourteenth ancient Olympiad, Diaulos, the double strade-race, was introduced as a new event. Hypenus of Pisa was the winner.

At the ancient fifteenth Olympiad, another new event, Dolichos—the long race, was introduced. Acanthus of Sparta was the winner in 720 B.C.

In 708 B.C. at the ancient eighteenth Olympiad, two more new events were introduced: pentathlon and wrestling. The pentathlon winner was Lampis of Sparta. The pentathlon consisted of discus and javelin throwing, a standing long jump, wrestling, and a short footrace. The wrestling winner was Eurytabus of Sparta.

At the ancient twenty-third Olympiad held in 688 B.C., a new event, boxing, was introduced. Onomastus of Smyrna was the winner.

The chariot race with teams of four horses, another new event, was introduced in 680 B.C. at the ancient twenty-fifth Olympiad. The winner of the chariot race was Pagondas of Thebes.

In 648 B.C. two new events were introduced at the thirty-third Olympiad; they were the pankration and the horse race. The pankration was regarded as a supreme test of courage, resourcefulness, skill, and strength. Lgdamus of Syracuse won the pankration. Cranxidas of Crannon won the horse race.

At the thirty-seventh Olympiad, two new events were introduced in 632 B.C.; they were the boys' footrace and wrestling. During this time, the Olympiad was extended from a single day of competition to five days, with two additional days devoted to religious ceremonies. The boys' footrace winner was Polynices of Sparta. The wrestling winner was Hipposthene of Sparta.

In 628 B.C. at the thirty-eighth Olympiad, the boys' pentathlon, a new event, was introduced. Eutelidas of Sparta won this event.

Boys' boxing was introduced in 616 B.C. at the forty-first Olympiad. The winner was Philyatis of Sybaris, from a wealthy Greek colony in Italy.

About 570 B.C., Eleans gained control of the Olympic Games. Around the sixty-first Olympiad, the winners were permitted to have statues erected in their honor in Olympia, after they had won three times.

In 540 B.C., Milo of Croton won the first of seven Olympic crowns. He won the wrestling crown at Olympia six times and was never defeated. It was said that he developed his strength by carrying a calf on his shoulders every day of his life until it was a full-grown bull.

In 520 B.C. at the sixty-fifth Olympiad, another new event was introduced, a race in armor (the hoplite race). The winner was Demaratus of Herala.

At the seventieth Olympiad in 500 B.C., a new event, the chariot race for mules, was introduced. Thersos of Thessaly won that event.

In 496 B.C. at the seventy-first Olympiad, another new event, the chariot race for mares, was introduced. The winner of the race was Pataicos of Dyma.

In 456 B.C., the Temple of Zeus at Olympia was completed. The ancient Greeks worshiped many gods in nearly every aspect of life. Zeus was the supreme god in charged of thunderstorms and tempests. The contestant at the Olympic Games swore his Olympic oath to play fair to Zeus.

In 435 B.C. sculptor Phidias completed the statue of Zeus in the temple at Olympia. In 408 B.C. the new event, a chariot race for teams of two horses, was introduced at the ninety-third Olympiad. Eugoras of Elis won that race.

At the ninety-sixth Olympiad in 396 B.C., two new events were introduced; they were the heralds and trumpeters. The winner of the contest for heralds was Timaios of Elis. The winner of the contest for trumpeters was Crater of Elis.

In 388 B.C. at the ninety-eighth Olympiad, another new event was introduced, the chariot race for teams of four colts. The winner of the race was Eurybiades of Sparta.

Between 365 and 364 B.C. Acadians invaded and took over the Olympia. The reign of Alexander the Great was between 336 and 323 B.C. and during his reign, the palm branch was introduced as an immediate symbol of victory in the Olympic Games.

At the 128th Olympiad in 268 B.C., a new event was introduced, the chariot race for teams of two colts. The race for colts was a new event introduced at the 131st Olympiad in 256 B.C.

In 200 B.C. at the 145th Olympiad, yet another new event was introduced. About 50 B.C., the first association of professional athletes was formed. In 12 B.C. Herod, King of Judea, presided over the Olympic Games.

At the 293rd Olympiad, Emperor Theodesius I abolished the Olympic Festival in A.D. 394 because he felt that the games had pagan connotations. Shortly after that, the historic city of the Olympia was looted and the colossal statue of Zeus was carried to Constantinople, where it was destroyed in a fire. Theodosius II in the fifth century A.D. issued orders to destroy all pagan temples. About A.D. 426, the Temple of Zeus at Olympia was destroyed by fire.

HISTORY OF THE MODERN OLYMPICS

Baron Pierre de Coubertin was the founder of the modern Olympic Games. He was a French aristocrat, scholar, and educator. Pierre de Coubertin was born in Paris on January 1, 1863. He was educated at a military academy in St. Cyr, but later decided to leave and study political science. From this field he became interested in national and international problems of education. He visited schools, colleges, and universities on the continent, in England, and the United States and decided that education and athletics could help develop better international understanding.

Baron de Coubertin felt that a well-rounded educational program should include athletics to balance the development of the mind and body, and that it would also lead to better cooperation among nations and peaceful competition. Coubertin decided that the Olympic Games should not be just for France but for the whole world, for universal understanding with amateurs competing on an equal basis. It was his feeling that wars were fought because nations misunderstand each other and peace could be obtained if prejudices that separate different races were eliminated. He felt that his ideals could be achieved by periodically bringing the youth of all countries together in competition to help increase international understanding.

Coubertin first publicly presented his idea about the Olympic Games to the Athletic Sports Union in Paris in 1892. At the international Athletic Congress in 1894, which was attended by representatives from many nations, he proposed that the Olympic Games be revived. His proposal was accepted and they all agreed to hold the first game in Athens, Greece, in April 1896.

In 1896, Coubertin founded the International Olympic Committee (IOC). The IOC was composed of two bodies: the Executive Board of the Executive Commission and the General Assembly. From out of the General Assembly the members of the Executive Board are elected. The Executive Board is composed of a president, two vice-presidents, and five members. The committee's six basic principles were (1) games would be held every four years, (2) contests would include modern sports, (3) competition would be limited to adult males, (4) only amateurs would be allowed to take part in the games, (5) the Olympics would move from city to city every four years, and (6) at least twelve countries must enter the competition.

Coubertin stated that: "The important thing in the Olympic Games is not to win but to take part, just as the important thing in life is not the triumph but the struggle. The essential thing is not to have conquered but to have fought well. To spread these percepts is to build up a stronger and more valiant and above all more scrupulous and more gracious humanity." The first two sentences of Coubertin's statement are used as the Olympic creed.

At the opening ceremonies, the Olympic flag is raised to the music of trumpets while pigeons and balloons are released. Then the Olympic flame, which has been carried from Olympia by a relay of runners (and ships and planes when necessary), is carried into the stadium, and the Olympic torch is lit. Then the Olympic hymn is sung and a contestant from the host country recites the Olympic Oath: "In the name of all competitors I promise that we will take part in these Olympic Games, respecting and abiding by the rules which govern them, in the true spirit of sportsmanship for the glory and the honor of our teams." The Olympic torch burns throughout the games and is extinguished at the closing ceremony.

The Olympic flame is not lit again until the next Olympic Games. The Olympic torch is the symbol of world friendship in sports. The Olympic flag has five colored rings linked together; every national flag in the world has at least one of these colors. The Olympic creed is displayed on the scoreboards at the Opening Ceremony of every Olympiad. These words express the hope that fair play and good sportsmanship will prevail throughout the games. The glow of the flame has also brought peoples from different countries together in a true Olympic spirit.

At the first modern Olympics, the first-place winners received a diploma, a silver medal, and a crown of olive branches. The second-place winner received a diploma, a bronze medal, and a crown of laurel. Now the first six winners in each event get diplomas. The first three prize winners also get medals: gold for first place, silver for second place, and bronze for third place. Prizes can only be won by teams and individuals, not the country.

Pierre de Coubertin headed the International Olympic Committee (IOC) until 1925, when he retired. He died in 1937.

Track and Field

Evelyn Ashford

EVELYN ASHFORD
(Born 1957—)

Evelyn Ashford in 1984 achieved an Olympic record and received a gold medal in the women's 100-meter run with a time of 10.97 seconds. Also in 1984 she received the gold medal in the women's 4 x 100-meter relay with a time of 41.65 seconds. And in 1988 Evelyn Ashford won a gold medal for the women's 4 x 100-meter relay with a time of 41.98 seconds and a silver medal for the women's 100-meter run with a time of 10.83 seconds.

Evelyn Ashford was born on April 15, 1957, in Shreveport, Louisiana. Her father is a sergeant in the Air Force, therefore as a child she and her brother and three sisters moved from place to place as a military family. Before she entered high school, her family had moved several times. They now live in Roseville, California, where her father is stationed at the McClellan Air Force Base. Evelyn attended Roseville High School.

Evelyn competed for the first time at age fourteen at the Junior Olympics in Washington. One of Evelyn's teachers was impressed by her athletic abilities and encouraged her to participate in track. She joined the boy's track team because there was not a team for girls at her high school. Running the 50-yard dash, Evelyn was able to beat the schools' star football player each time they competed. She gained regional and statewide recognition during high school and received one of UCLA's first athletic scholarships to women in 1975.

Evelyn gained prominence while a freshman at UCLA, where she finished second in the 100 meters, made the Olympic team, and finished fifth at the Montreal Olympics. Evelyn met Pat Connolly at UCLA, who became her coach for the next ten years.

During this ten-year period, Evelyn married Ray Washington, who was an assistant basketball coach at San Jacinto College. During her career she accomplished dual goals: a world's record and an Olympic gold medal.

She decided to quit college, because she had become disinterested in pursuing her studies and the athletic scholarship did not pay for her books and other necessities of college life. She left UCLA in 1979 and went to work in a Nike shoe store, so that she would have time to concentrate on being able to compete on a world-class level. Pat, her coach, volunteered to continue coaching her, even though she was no longer a student at UCLA. In 1979 Evelyn was considered the best sprinter in the world, winning the 100-meter and 200-meter races at the World Cup in Montreal and set the American 200-meter record of 21.83 seconds. She defeated East Germans Marlies Gohr and Marita Koch in the World Class Invitational.

She had to drop out of the U.S. Olympics in 1980 because of a pulled hamstring muscle. She went home to her husband, that summer they took a car trip, and she made some decisions about her future. She decided to enter California State University to study fashion design and to prepare for the 1984 Olympics. She still had dreams of winning a gold medal, so she decided to try for it again. She also decided to let her husband become her coach. In 1981 Evelyn won the World Cup in sprints and in 1983 she beat Marlies Gohr again.

In 1983 she set the world's record at a Zurich meet and in 1984 was chosen Athlete of the Year. She was the first Olympic female winner to have ever run faster than 10.97 seconds in the 100-meter dash. In February 1986, Evelyn won the 55-meter dash in 6.6 seconds at the Vitalis Olympic Invitational.

Finally, she began to enjoy the economic benefits that comes with winning the gold medal. The American Express Company ran full-page color advertisements in national magazines showing Evelyn running barefoot across a California desert. The ad indicated that she had been a "card member since 1983." The Mazda Automobile Company paid her a promotional fee to join its track team and become a spokeswoman for the company. She became a reporter for "World Class Woman," a cable television program about female athletes.

In May 1985, Evelyn gave birth to her daughter, Raina Ashby Washington. Evelyn felt that motherhood made her a better runner, because it improved her endurance. During pregnancy, the female is carrying an average of twenty-five additional pounds, which will strengthen the legs and the heart rate. The stroke volume rises, increasing the amount of blood the heart pumps, which improves fitness and endurance.

In 1988 at the XXIV Olympiad in Seoul, Korea, she won two more medals: a gold in the 400-meter relay and a silver in the 100-meter dash. Her dreams of receiving a gold medal and having a baby had finally become reality.

Track and Field

Valerie Brisco-Hooks

VALERIE BRISCO-HOOKS
(Born 1960—   )

Valerie Brisco-Hooks in 1984 became the first American woman ever to win an Olympic gold medal in both the 200- and 400-meter runs and the second woman ever to win three gold medals at the Olympics. At the XXIII Olympiad in 1984 in Rome, Italy, she received gold medals in the 400-meter run, which she completed in 48.83 seconds; in the 200-meter run, which she completed in 21.81 seconds; and she ran the third leg in the 1,600-meter relay that ran 3:18:29.

Valerie Brisco was born on July 6, 1960, in Greenwood, Mississippi. She was the sixth of ten children born to Arguster and Guitherea Brisco. When Valerie was five years old her family moved to Los Angeles, California.

Valerie attended Locke High School in Los Angeles, Califoria, where she was recognized as having natural athletic ability. Her inspirations for track came from a high school teacher, who recommended that she read about Wilma Rudolph, and her brother, Robert, who in 1974 was killed by a stray bullet while running on the school's track field at age eighteen. In 1977, while still in high school, she ran the 400 meters in 54.19 seconds.

After graduation, she attended California State in Northridge, where she met Bob Kersee and he became her coach. In 1979, Valerie joined the World Class Track Team, where she became recognized as an AIAW champion and an AAU runner-up in the 200-meter race. Also in 1979 she ran the 400 meters in 52.08 seconds and set an American record of 49.83 seconds in the TAC Championships.

While attending California State in 1979, Valerie met Alvin

Hooks and two-and-half years later they were married. In 1981 her husband was drafted by the Philadelphia Eagles football team as a wide receiver, so they left California to live in Philadelphia. In 1982 she gave birth to their son, Alvin Hooks, Jr. In 1983, she continued her training with Bob Kersee. In 1984, Alvin and Valerie divorced, after separations and attempts at reconciliation.

In 1984 at the Olympics in Rome, Valerie made history by winning three gold medals for the 200 meters, 400 meters, and the 1,600-meter relay. She also lowered the American record and broke the Olympic record. In 1985, with her former husband serving as her coach, she ranked second in the 200-meter dash and third in the 400-meter dash. In 1986 she finished third in the 200- and 400-meter dashes and fifth in the world. In 1987 she won the U.S. Olympic Festival, but finished fourth at the TAC. In 1988 she ran the third leg in the 1,600-meter relay to win a silver medal at 3:15:51. At the Pan American Games in Indianapolis, Indiana, after she won a gold medal for the 1,600-meter relay, a deaf teenager asked her to pose with him for a picture. Before the picture was taken, she took her gold medal off and put it around his neck and after the picture was taken, she smiled and walked away, leaving the medal with the teenager.

Taking care of her son was her top priority and Valerie gave it up for a period of time to achieve her goal to become a winner.

Track and Field

Earlene Brown

EARLENE BROWN
(Born 1935—Died 1983)

Earlene Brown has been recognized by many as one of the greatest athletes ever to qualify for the finals in the shot put for three consecutive Olympics in 1956, 1960, and 1964. In 1960 at the XVII Olympiad in Rome, Italy, she placed third and received a bronze medal for the shot put with a score of 53 feet, 10½ inches.

She was born Earlene Dennis on July 11, 1935, in Latero, Texas. She was an only child. At the age of three, Earlene's mother left her father. At a very early age, Earlene started playing sports. She was considered by many to have natural athletic abilities, because she won many of her competitions without much training. Earlene's father played semipro baseball in Texas for many years, so she may have inherited her athletic abilities from her father. Earlene had a love for competitve sports. When she was about ten years old, she began traveling with a softball team as a catcher.

Earlene began her participation in track and field activities as a member of DAP, the California equivalent of the Police League in New York City, where she was able to participate in the citywide track meets in Los Angeles, California. She participated in the 100-yard dash. She anchored the relay team. And she competed in the basketball throw. She was later taught by two of her teachers how to shot put and use the discus. Earlene won four gold medals and a trophy for baseball and basketball throws and for the discus and the shot put.

After graduating from high school, Earlene went to Compton Junior College. She got married and gave birth to a son, Reggie. In 1956, at twenty-one years old, Earlene joined the AAU and

35

became the new American record holder in both the shot put and in the discus. At the Philadephia AAU outdoor nationals she set a new American record of 45 feet and placed second in the discus. Also in 1956, at the XVI Olympiad in Melbourne, Australia, Earlene placed third on the U.S. Olympic team with a shot put score of 46 feet, 6½ inches. Later that same afternoon she reclaimed her title with a shot put of 46 feet, 9½ inches. She later set a new American record of 46 feet, 11 inches. Earlene became a double winner in the Olympic Trials.

For a while Earlene's husband tried to work as her coach, but they soon realized that this coaching was not increasing her skills. As Earlene achieved fame, problems increased in their marriage. Later she and her husband separated. Her mother tried to support Earlene in all of her endeavors. She took care of Earlene's son while Earlene participated in different sport competitions.

In 1957 at the AAU outdoor nationals held in Cleveland, Ohio, Earlene placed second in the discus throw. She won the championship for the shot put for two consecutive years.

In 1958 Earlene established a new American record in the Basketball throw with a score of 135 feet, 2 inches, which was thirty feet beyond the old record. Also in 1958 in Monmouth, New Jersey, she broke her old American record and won first place with a score of 47 feet, 5½ inches in the shot put. She won a gold medal in the discus with a throw of 152 feet, 5½ inches. In August 1958, Earlene competed in Europe and won two gold medals and set a new record of 54 feet, 3½ inches in the shot put. She was recognized by the Associated Press as the "toast of Moscow." In 1958, at the dual meet between the U.S.S.R. and the United States held in Philadelphia, she placed second in the shot put with a score of 51 feet, 6½ inches. In the discus she finished in third place with a throw of 161 feet, 1½ inches.

In 1959 in Chicago, Illinois, at the Pan American Games, Earlene set a new meet record in both the shot put and the discus. Her discus record was 153 feet, 8 inches. In Athens, Greece, at the Panathenian Stadium, she threw the discus 155 feet, 8¾ inches; this throw went out of the stadium, up into the stands, and hit two people. Earlene won first place in the shot put and won the national championships in the discus and shot put in the United States. She became the only American women to ever shot put over 50 feet. Earlene placed second in the discus with 162 feet. In Warsaw, Poland, she won two more gold medals for placing first in the shot put and the discus.

At the Olympic Trials meet in Abilene, Earlene set a new record of 176 feet, 10½ inches. Her shot put was 50 feet, 10 inches, which made her a double winner; and she set a new Olympic record that broke her own 1956 record. At Corpus Christi, Earlene won the international championships in the discus and shot put.

At the U.S.A. Relay Championship in Buffalo, New York, Earlene won the discus throw with over 171 feet and she won a gold medal for the javelin throw of 118 feet. She made the U.S. Women's Olympic team in Rome, Italy. She acted as mother to all of her teammates, of whom eleven were African-Americans and five white. Earlene also organized the Olympic Village dancing and card games. She won third place in the shot put and sixth place in the discus. Three weeks later in Frankfort, Germany, in a dual meet with the Germans, Earlene set a new American record with a shot put of 54 feet, 9 inches.

In the British Commonwealth Games in London, Earlene won the shot put and the discus. She returned to the Panathenian Stadium in Athens, Greece, and threw the discus over 171 feet. At the AAU Outdoor Nationals she placed first in the shot put and the discus. She was chosen to represent the United States on its tour of Europe, but Earlene could not go because she had just purchased a beauty salon.

In 1962 Earlene was considered a great American star when she beat Russia's athlete in Moscow. That same year she competed in the AAU Outdoor Nationals, which were held in Los Angeles, California. Because she was not able to train as much as needed, she barely qualified—finishing in fifth place. In the finals she won the national championships with a score of 48 feet, 10½ inches in the shot put and placed second in the discus.

In 1963, once again because Earlene did not have the needed time to train, she lost the AAU Outdoor National title in the shot put. She was not chosen to represent the United States in the Pan American Games.

In 1964 in Hanford, California, at the outdoor nationals, Earlene won first place in the shot put with a score of 46 feet, 11 inches and placed second in the discus with 156 feet, 8 inches. That year in the dual meet between the Soviet Union and the United States, she placed third in the shot put and placed fourth in the discus. Also in 1964, Earlene made a comeback and qualified for a third time for a place on the U.S. Women's Olympic team. She did not win any medals in the Olympics in Tokyo, Japan, but she became the only athlete in the world to reach the finals in the shot put for three consecutive years at the Olympics. Because of Earlene's popularity, she was still recognized by many as one of the great American athletes of all time. Earlene won a gold medal in the shot put and a silver medal in the discus at the Japan, United States, and British Commonwealth Games in Osaka, Japan.

Earlene felt very happy to have had an opportunity to participate in sports, which was her love, and to have a chance to see the world. After she retired from amateur sports, Earlene became a superstar in the roller derby. She died in 1983.

Track and Field

Chandra Cheeseborough

CHANDRA CHEESEBOROUGH
(Born 1959—   )

Chandra Cheeseborough was a three-time Olympian—she received three medals at the XXIII Olympiad in Los Angeles, California. At the 1984 Olympics she received a gold medal as a member of the 4 x 100-meter relay with a time of 41.65 seconds, a gold medal as a member of the the 4 x 400-meter relay and helped set a new Olympic record of 3:18.29, and a silver medal for placing second in the 400-meter run with a time of 49.05 seconds.

Chandra was born on January 10, 1959, in Jacksonville, Florida. She attended Ribault High School in Jacksonville, Florida, where she participated in their track program. At the age of sixteen, she participated in the Pan American Games and set a Florida sprint record.

In 1976 Chandra won the TAC 100-meter title and earned the tenth place world ranking in the 100 meters. She was recognized as one of the most versatile sprinters and one of the best 400-meter runners in the world. In 1984 she placed second in the 400-meter run at the Olympics.

Chandra's interest was in health and physical education. Winning was very important to her because she felt that people do not talk about a loser. They just remember the ones who are on top. Chandra would like for people to remember her name when she is not around.

Track and Field

Alice Coachman

ALICE COACHMAN
(Born 1923—   )

Alice Coachman in 1948 became the first African-American woman to win an Olympic gold medal when she placed first in the high jump competition at the XIV Olympiad in London, England, and the first American woman to win a gold medal in track and field. With this jump, Alice, along with Dorothy Tyler of Great Britain, set a new Olympic record of 5 feet, 6¼ inches, but Alice was awarded the gold medal because she had fewer misses.

Alice Coachman was born on November 9, 1923, in Albany, Georgia. She was the daughter of Fred and Evelyn Jackson Coachman. Alice attended Monroe Street Elementary School, where she developed a love for sports. On the playground she and her girl friends would jump over rope to see how high they could jump. She would beat all of them, so she decided to compete against the boys and would also beat them. This kind of play worried her parents, because it was not fashionable or ladylike for females to participate in sports. Alice's interest in the high jump materialized when she attended a boys' track and field meet.

At Madison High School she was encouraged to participate in sports. The summer of 1939, Alice was invited to attend Tuskegee Preparatory School, where she broke the high school and collegiate high-jump records. When she was sixteen years old, she left Albany, Georgia, to attend Tuskegee Institute High School in Tuskegee, Alabama, where she set many records. Her performance at the national Amateur Athletic Union (AAU) meets for Tuskegee Institute contributed to its reputation in women's track and field. The Tuskegee Relays were the proving ground for many young African-American females in the south.

45

For about ten years, Alice participated in the different competitions. Alice won first place in the AAU high jump and from 1939 to 1948 she won in the high jump. From 1941 to 1943, she won the U.S. indoor title, eight AAU sprint titles outdoors, and two indoors. From 1943 to 1947, she won the U.S. outdoor 50-meter dash and the 100-meter dash in 1942, 1945, and 1946. It was in Waterburg, Connecticut, that Alice won her first medal. At Tuskegee she also excelled in basketball and was an All-American guard.

In 1946, Alice received her trade degree in dressmaking from Tuskegee Institute. In 1947, she transferred to Albany State College to continue her academic and athletic careers. In 1948, she was invited to join the American team for the London Olympics. Alice was the only one from the American women's team to win a gold medal.

When she returned to America, she was introduced to President Harry S. Truman, a parade was given in her honor, a ceremony has held, she was given a motorcade ride from Atlanta to Macon, and her sorority—Delta Sigma Theta—gave her a banquet. After winning this victory she decided to retire from sports competition and the limelight.

In 1949, she graduated from Albany State College with a major in home economics and a minor in science. Alice started teaching high school physical education in Albany, Georgia. She married N. F. Davis and later divorced him. They had one son and a daughter. With her background in home economics, science, and sports, she was able to work at South Carolina State College, Albany State College, and Tuskegee High School.

In 1981 Alice was featured in a documentary film. She was inducted into the National Track and Field Hall of Fame, the Helm's Hall of Fame, the Tuskegee Hall of Fame, and the Georgia Hall of Fame. She was also a teacher at the Turner Job Corps Center in Albany, Georgia.

Alice is now retired and married again to Frank Davis and they live in Tuskegee, Alabama.

Track and Field

Isabelle Daniel

ISABELLE DANIEL
(Born 1937—   )

Isabelle Daniel made the 1956 U.S. Olympic track and field team after winning the 100-meter run in the Olympic tryouts held in Washington, D.C. At the XVI Olympiad held in Melbourne, Australia, she won a bronze medal as a member of the U.S. relay team. The U.S. team won third place at the Olympics.

Isabelle Daniel was born on July 31, 1937, in Jakin, Georgia. She was the youngest of nine children; there were five girls and four boys. Her father was a school bus driver and a farmer. Her mother was a teacher. Isabelle's parents taught their children to use the talents that they were blessed with. Her father realized she had athletic ability when she was about five or six years old. Her brothers were trying to catch a pig in their garden. They were having a hard time so Isabelle asked her father if she could try to catch the pig. Her father gave her permission, so she ran and caught up with the pig and passed it. They realized that running was her calling. Isabelle would race against two of her brothers and she would always beat them.

At age sixteen Isabelle was recognized as a sprint star. She wanted to make a good impression at the 1954 upcoming relay at Tuskegee, so her father allowed her to run alongside the school bus on its way to school everyday. Her home was thirteen miles from the school. Isabelle was encouraged by her older brothers to run and play basketball. She was encouraged by other people in her community and by her teachers to compete in sports. She competed in some county meets and the state competitions. Isabelle won two or three events within about two or three years.

In Isabelle's senior year while running at the Tuskegee Relay,

Mr. Temple, a coach from Tennessee State University, noticed her. He liked her running style and invited her to attend the summer clinic at Tennessee State University. He taught her the fundamentals of running and how to start from the blocks instead of from a standing start. She improved so much that summer that she was able to win the junior nationals.

In addition to playing sports in high school, Isabelle was a cheerleader and was the school's "Miss Carver High School" in Early County. She graduated from high school as an honor student and received a work-aid scholarship to attend Tennessee State University. In 1954 in Harrisburg, Pennsylvania, at the National AAU Women's Track and Field Championships, she was a member of the winning 800-meter relay team.

Isabelle was a member of the winning 660-yard medley relay team in the Alabama State Relays at Montgomery, Alabama, in 1955. In Morristown, New Jersey, in 1955, she made a noteworthy performance in the 50-meter dash. Also in 1955, Isabelle won the 50-yard dash in the National AAU Track and Field Championships at Ponca City, Oklahoma, and she set a new American girls' outdoor record.

In 1956 in Philadelphia, Pennsylvania, at the National AAU Women's Track and Field Championships, Isabelle was a member of the winning 400-meter relay team. In 1957 she was part of the U.S.A. All-time Indoor Top Ten in the 100-yard dash. Isabelle won the 220-yard dash in the AAU National Indoor Championships in Shaker Heights, Ohio, in 1957.

Isabelle placed third in the 200-meter dash as a member of the national team in the U.S.-U.S.S.R. competition in Moscow, Russia, in 1958. She won the 60-meter dash in the Pan American Games in Chicago, Illinois, in 1959 and set a new American and games' record.

Isabelle won the AAU All-American in 1957, 1958, and 1959. She won the 60-meter dash in the National Women's Track and Field Championships in Cleveland, Ohio, in 1959 and set an American record in the trials. Isabelle won the 200-meter dash in the National AAU Women's Track and Field Championships in Cleveland, Ohio, in 1959 and set a new meet record.

Isabelle was a member of the winning 400-meter relay team in the Olympic Games in Rome, Italy, in 1960 and she helped the team set a new world's and Olympic record. Isabelle was one of the first women to hold a record at the AAU Senior Championships. In five years of national and international competition, Isabelle participated in more than twenty-five meets and won more than a hundred awards.

Isabelle graduated from Tennessee State University and started teaching at Carver High School in Columbus, Ohio. She met and later married Sidney Holston. They have four children, two girls and two boys. All of their children followed in her footsteps and participated in sports. Neither she nor her husband forced their children into athletics. Still, each one attempted to play athletics for a brief period. Their oldest son, Sidney, ran track, but earned a basketball scholarship. Frederick played football up to the B-team level. Inessa started running track, but settled on a sideline role to support the athletic program. And Kezia ran track for three years before she was ten years old, but decided to play basketball.

Isabelle is a teacher at McNair Junior High School and a coach for the girls at McNair High School. Isabelle's girls' track teams have won four state, twelve regional, and seven county championships.

In 1987 Isabelle was inducted into the Georgia Hall of Fame along with seven males. She was the only female included in that year's selection. Isabelle said she equates the Hall of Fame honor with that of the Nobel Prize or the Oscars. She said it was a thrilling feeling and a great honor.

Isabelle was selected the Track Coach of the Year by the National High School Athletic Coaches Association. She was nominated in 1985 for this honor and was chosen from a group of eight nominees, one from each region in the country. Region III includes Alabama, Georgia, Florida, Kentucky, North Carolina, South Carolina, and Tennessee. She was nominated for the national honor after being named the Region III coach of the year. She said being selected coach of the year was the thrill of her life. She said that this award meant more to her than anything else. She said that there is no comparison with other honors, because this award stands for how much she has helped others in return for how much others have always helped her. Isabelle recognizes the fact that this wouldn't have been possible without her students and their never-quit spirit and the support of her family and co-workers. She said that track is her sport and she enjoys coaching as much or even more than competing.

Isabelle said she always wanted to coach and to inspire kids. She tells her students, "Don't quit, don't give up. Do the best you can, regardless of the outcome. If you really want it, you'll stay out there and the rewards will come."

Isabelle still resides in Decatur, Georgia, with her husband, Sidney, and is very involved with the 1996 Olympics, which will be held in Atlanta, Georgia.

Track and Field

Gail Devers

GAIL DEVERS
(Born 1967—   )

Gail Devers in 1993 was one of the athletes named the "1993 Athlete of the Year" by the U.S. Olympic Committee. At the XXV Olympiad in 1992 in Barcelona, Spain, she won the women's 100-meter run by one-hundredth of a second. Her finishing time was 10.82 seconds.

Gail Devers grew up in San Diego, California, with her mother, father, and brother. Her father, Rev. Larry Devers, is associate minister of Mount Erie Baptist Church in San Diego, California. Her mother, Alabe, was an elementary school teacher's aide. Gail's brother, Parenthesis, is fourteen months older than she is.

Gail started running track in high school as a distance runner. In 1984 at the California high school track championships, Gail won the 100 meters and the 100-meter hurdles and finished second in the long jump. That same year she enrolled at UCLA and Bob Kersee became her coach. Because of his faith in her ability, she began to believe in herself.

In 1988 Gail set an American record in the 100-meter hurdles. Because of this record, she made the Olympic team for the 100-meter hurdles in Seoul, Korea. Her performance was poor, therefore she failed to make the finals. Shortly afterward, she developed a mysterious illness that was misdiagnosed as diabetes and exhaustion.

For almost two years Gail suffered vision loss in her left eye, fluctuation in her weight, uncontrollable shaking, and continuous menstrual bleeding. Finally she was diagnosed as having Graves' disease, which is a thyroid disorder. It could be controlled with medication but Gail decided not to take it because it was on the banned medications list for the Olympics. The other treatment for the disease is radiation, so she decided to go through that. The radiation destroyed the cyst, as well as the whole thyroid gland. Her feet began to swell and ooze a yellow fluid and her skin began to crack and bleed. The pain was so intense that her parents had to carry her to the bathroom. They were afraid that her feet would have to be amputated, but the doctors realized that she was having a reaction to the radiation. The treatments were changed and within a month she was able to walk again.

Gail continued her training with Bob Kersee, and at the TAC 1991 World Championship in Tokyo, Japan, she received a silver medal in the 100-meter hurdles. In 1992 she won the Barcelona Olympic 100-meter dash, but in the 100-meter hurdles she tripped, dived across the line, and placed fifth. But the big victory for Gail was overcoming the debilitating effects of Graves' disease and winning the 100-meter competition for women with a finishing score of 10.82 seconds.

Gail is married and would like to open a day care center so she can teach young children.

Track and Field

Mae Faggs

MAE FAGGS
(Born 1932—   )

Mae Faggs became the first African-American woman from the United States to have participated in three different Olympics. She made the 1948, 1952, and the 1956 Olympic teams. She was the youngest member of the 1948 team. In 1952 at the XV Olympiad in Helsinki, Finland, Mae was a member of the winning 4 x 100-meter relay team with a time of 45.9 seconds and received a gold medal. In 1956 she received a bronze medal as a member of the 4 x 100-meter relay team in Melbourne, Australia, at the XVI Olympiad with a time of 44.9 seconds. In Mae's ten years of competition she won twenty-six trophies, three plaques, one hundred medals, and ten certificates. She held every American sprint record, indoors and outdoors, as well as running anchor on world's and American record-breaking relay teams.

Mae Heriwentha Faggs was born on April 10, 1932, in Mays Landing, New Jersey. She and her brother lived with their parents. When Mae was in the seventh or eighth grade, a policeman came to her elementary school because he was looking for some boys to run in a track meet that was being sponsored by the Police Athletic League. When the boys were running, Mae told the patrolman that she could outrun the boys. She was given an opportunity to prove her claim and she did. She was then given the opportunity to join the girl's team from the 11th Precinct in Bayside, Long Island. Later Sergeant John Brennan decided to start an AAU team and told Mae that she would be going to the Olympics. He entered her in the 1948 trials for the U.S. Olympic team, which was being held in Providence, Rhode Island. Mae made the team.

After graduating from high school Mae received a work-aid scholarship to Tennessee State University. When she arrived at the university, the women's track team had a poor rating. Mae became an individual star, she won all the sprint events. She was the person who kept the team in top condition and at its competitive best. She had team spirit and demanded the same from her teammates.

In 1949 in New York, New York, Mae became the holder of the 200-meter dash indoor record. Also the same year, she won and set an American record in the 220-yard dash in New York, New York.

In 1952 in Buffalo, New York, Mae set an American indoor record in the 100-meter dash. That year, she was a member of the winning 880-yard U.S. national relay team in London, England. And she was also a member of the winning 400-meter relay team in the Helsinki Olympic Games in Helsinki, Finland.

At the National AAU Women's Championships in Harrisburg, Pennsylvania, in 1953 Mae won the 100-yard dash and set an AAU championship record. In 1954 in Harrisburg, Pennsylvania, she was a member of the winning 800-meter relay team in the National AAU Women's Championships.

In 1955 Mae won the 100-meter dash in the Evening Star Games in Washington, D.C. She became the first Tennessee State University woman athlete to win an Olympic gold medal in Chicago, Illinois. At the same Olympics, Mae was a member of the winning 400-meter relay team. Also in 1955, she was awarded gold track shoes from Tennessee State University. She became the holder of the 100-yard dash record at the AAU Women's Senior Indoor Championships. In Montgomery, Alabama, at the Alabama State Relays, Mae won the 100-yard dash. At the same relay, she was a member of the winning 440- and the 660-yard relay teams. And Mae also won the 220-yard dash in the Alabama State Relays.

At the National AAU Women's Championship in Ponca City, Oklahoma, in 1955 Mae was a member of the winning 440-relay team and set an AAU Championship record. Mae was a member of the U.S. Olympic team at the 1956 Olympic Games, which were held in Melbourne, Australia. In Helsinki, Finland, she won a bronze medal in the 100-yard dash in the Olympic Games.

Mae was named AAU All-American for three years: 1954, 1955, and 1956. In 1956 in Philadelphia, Pennsylvania, Mae was a member of the winning 480-meter relay team at the National AAU Women's Championships and helped set an AAU Championship record.

In 1965 Mae was elected to the Helms Hall of Fame. In 1975 she was inducted into the National Track and Field Hall of Fame in Charleston, West Virginia.

Mae graduated from Tennessee State University and decided to go to the University of Cincinnati to get a master's degree in special education. She started teaching school in Cincinnati. She married Eddie Starr, who was a high school principal. Mae is very active in promoting youth programs in Cincinnati, Ohio.

Track and Field

Barbara Ferrell

BARBARA FERRELL
(Born 1947—   )

Barbara Ferrell placed second in the 100-meter run at the XIX Olympiad in Mexico City, Mexico. She received the silver medal. At the same Olympics, Barbara received a gold medal as a member of the winning 4 x 100-meter relay team and helped the team set an Olympic and world's record of 42.8 seconds.

Barbara Ann Ferrell was born on July 28, 1947, in Hattiesburg, Mississippi. She attended Harrison Technical High School in Chicago, Illinois. Barbara won the Illinois State Championship 60-meter dash. After graduating from high school, she enrolled in Los Angeles City College. She became a member of the Girls Athletic Association in Chicago and a member of the Los Angeles Mercurettes.

In 1967 in Santa Barbara, Barbara became AAU champion in the 100-meter dash with a time of 11.1 seconds. She held the American 200-meter record with 22.8 seconds in the Olympics in 1968. The same year at the Pan American Games, Barbara won the 100-meter dash and received a gold medal with a time of 11.5 seconds.

In 1969 Barbara won the national titles in the 100- and 200-meter dashes. In 1967 and 1969 she was the top-ranked U.S. women's sprinter in the 100-meter dash.

In 1972 Barbara won the Olympic trials in the 100-meter dash, but because of an injury, she finished seventh in both the 100- and 200-meter dashes at the Munich Games. This same year she ran fifth in the AAU 100-meter dash.

Barbara graduated from California State in 1969 with a Bachelor of Arts degree in sociology with a minor in education. She married Warren Edmondson and they live in Inglewood, California. They have two daughters, Malika and Maya. Barbara works as an area representaive for the Central Area Teachers in Los Angeles and is a member of the International Track Association.

Track and Field

Benita Fitzgerald-Brown

BENITA FITZGERALD-BROWN
(Born 1961—   )

Benita Fitzgerald-Brown in 1984 won the 100-meter hurdles in 12.84 seconds. At the XXIII Olympiad at Los Angeles, California, she won a gold medal.

Benita was born on July 6, 1961, in Warrenton, Virginia. A portion of her life was spent in Woodbridge, Virginia, and she attended Garfield High School. While in high school she was a member of the National Honor Society, played the flute and piccolo, and ran track.

Benita became interested in track when she was in the seventh grade and participated in the Presidential Physical Fitness tests and was asked by the physical education teacher to try out for the track team. From 1976 to 1979 she was Virginia State Champion. From 1978 to 1979 she was recognized as the U.S.A. Junior National Champion and fifteen times as All-American.

After graduation from high school, Benita became a freshman at the University of Tennessee in Knoxville, Tennessee, with a major in industrial engineering. In 1980 she became a member of the Olympic team and in 1981 became AIAW champion. In 1982 Benita won the NCAA title in the sprints with a time of 11.36 seconds in the 100 meters, and she was ranked tenth in the world. In 1983 her score in the 200 meters was 23.0 seconds, she placed eighth at the World Championships, and she maintained her tenth-place rank in the world. In 1984, Benita won a gold medal for the 100-meter hurdles, with a time of 12.84 seconds.

Benita is married to Laron Brown and they reside in Dale City, Virginia.

Tennis

Zina Garrison

ZINA GARRISON
(Born 1963—   )

Zina Garrison was the first black player to win the junior singles championship at Wimbledon. At the XXIV Olympiad in Seoul, Korea, she won a gold medal for doubles tennis and a bronze medal in singles tennis. Also, she was the first African-American woman to play at Wimbledon since Althea Gibson in 1958 and in 1988 was a member of the first U.S. Olympic tennis team since 1924. Zina became the first black to rank in the top ten since the women's pro tennis tour began in 1971.

Zina Garrison was born on November 16, 1963, in Houston, Texas. During the summer of 1963, Zina's mother had gone to the doctor because of the swelling she was experiencing and he told her she had a tumor. She sought a second opinion and found out she was pregnant with Zina.

Zina was the seventh child born to Mary and Ulysses Garrison. Zina's father, who was a postman, died from a stroke before she was a year old. She was named Zina for the end of the alphabet. Her four sisters called her Tumorlina. She was raised by her mother on the south side of Houston in a predominantly black working-class neighborhood. Her mother worked as an aide in a nursing home to support the family.

Zina's brothers and sisters spoiled her because they were so much older than she was. She was quiet and said to have a sense of clairvoyance, so she was also called the "Vision Girl." She grew up as a tomboy.

Zina loved to run, dance, and play softball. She would often follow her brother, Rodney, around. She became interested in tennis when she was between nine and ten years old while watching

73

her brother's girlfriend take tennis lessons at MacGregor Park, located in her neighborhood. To Zina, tennis was a combination of running, dancing, and batting all in one sport. John Wilkerson, a tennis pro, gave her a tennis racquet and after a few months, he was impressed with her talent so he became her coach.

From age ten to sixteen she competed in many local tournaments and by age sixteen she was playing in national tournaments. In 1979 she won the National Hard Court Doubles Championship for sixteen and under. In 1980 Zina won the National Girls Singles Championship. In 1981 at Wimbledon and the U.S. Open, she was the first African-American player to win the junior singles championship. That same year at the U.S. Open she won the junior singles title.

Zina received many honors in recognition of her accomplishments. The U.S. Olympic Committee named her Top Female Amateur Athlete in Tennis. From the International Tennis Federation, she received the Junior of the Year Award. The U.S. Tennis Association awarded her the Girls' Sportsmanship Trophy. On January 6, 1982, in Washington, D.C., it was proclaimed "Zina Garrison Day." By the end of this same year, Zina became a professional and was ranked number sixteen in the world of tennis.

In 1983 Zina's mother became ill from a diabetic reaction, which caused her to slip into a coma. Two days later her mother died. Zina and her mother were very close. She had shared the same bed with her mother until she was sixteen and they shared every confidence. She could not accept her mother's death. For months she pretended that her mother was on a long trip and tried to use food to fill the void. Zina became lonely and depressed and began food binges, devouring bags of cookies, boxes of cereal, cartons of ice cream in a single sitting. She would then be disgusted with herself and force herself to vomit. This pattern developed into bulimia, which she hid for many years. One day while she was training in Houston, she confided in her trainer, who recommended that Zina talk to a counselor.

She found out from therapy that her bulimia was caused by the three deaths in her immediate family: her father who died eleven months after she was born; her older brother (Willie Garrison), who was catcher with the Milwaukee Braves' minor league organization and was struck in the left eye by a ball and developed a fatal tumor; and the death of her mother. Finally Zina accepted her mother's death and begain to gain control and understand who she was.

Zina continued playing tennis and in 1988 at the Olympics in Seoul, Korea, she won a gold medal in the doubles and a bronze medal in the singles. Also in 1988, she became a member of the Federation Cup team and captain of the Wightman Cup team. In 1989 at the U.S. Open, Zina defeated Chris Evert during Chris's last tournament with a score of 7-6, 6-2. On September 23, 1989, Zina married Willard Jackson, a Houston businessman who founded a hazardous-waste disposal company. Her husband has become a very positive and supportive force in her life. He has been able to draw out Zina's feelings without overwhelming her. Her marriage seems to have added to her success in tennis.

Track and Field

Florence Griffith-Joyner

FLORENCE GRIFFITH-JOYNER
(Born 1959—   )

Florence Griffith-Joyner in 1988 became the first American woman to win four medals in a single Olympics. At the XXIV Olympiad in 1988 at Seoul, Korea, she won a gold medal in the 100-meter run and set an Olympic record of 10.54 seconds; a gold medal in the 200-meter run with a time of 21.34 seconds; a gold medal in the 4 x 100-meter relay with a time of 41.98 seconds; and a silver medal in the 1,600-meter relay, where she anchored the U.S. team and helped set an American record of 3:15.51. She became known as "the world's fastest woman." Her fans called her Flo Jo and it is felt by many that she brought glamour to the women's track and field events with her outfits and long, multi-colored painted fingernails.

Delorez Florence Griffith was born on December 21, 1959, in Los Angeles, California. She was the seventh of eleven children born to Robert and Florence Griffith. Florence was named after her mother, and at home she was called Dee Dee. Her father was an electronics technician and her mother was a seamstress. In 1963, Florence's mother separated from her father when Florence was four years old and moved with her eleven children from their house in the southern California desert to the Jordan Downs housing project in Watts. There were days when there was no food and other days when they only had oatmeal for breakfast, lunch, and dinner.

At age seven, Florence began running track through a program at the Sugar Ray Robinson Youth Foundation, a program funded for underprivileged youth. She continued competing in the 50- and 70-meter dashes while in elementary and high school. At age fourteen, Florence won the Jesse Owens National Youth Games and a trip to a San Francisco meet. The next year she won the same meet, she met and was congratulated by Jesse Owens, but was later informed that because of the rules she could not compete in the sectional competition in Texas because she had won the year before.

Florence attended Jordan High School in Los Angeles, California, and continued to set records in sprinting and long jumping. After she graduated from high school in 1978, the following fall she enrolled at California State University in Northridge with a major in business. Florence dropped out of college because she did not have enough money to pay her tuition and to purchase books. So she began working as a bank teller. Later, Bob Kersee, who was an assistant track coach at the university, had recognized her athletic abilities and helped her to apply for financial aid so she could continue her academic and athletic careers.

In 1980 her coach, Bob Kersee, took an assistant coaching position at UCLA. Even though UCLA did not offer a major in business and she had a 3.25-grade point average at California State, hesitantly she decided to change universities so she could continue her training with him. With her coach's help she received an athletic scholarship and changed her major to psychology. While at UCLA on the Westwood campus, Florence won the National Collegiate Athletic Association (NCAA) 200-meter championship in 1982 with a time of 22.39 seconds. In 1983, in the NCAA's 400-meter championship, she won. She also placed second in the 200 meters. She graduated in 1983 from UCLA with a major in psychology.

Florence continued competing and became known for her flamboyant clothes, nails, and hair. In 1984 at the XXIII Olympiad in Los Angeles, California, she won a silver medal in the 200-meter race.

After the Olympic Games, Florence retired from athletic competition between September 1986 and April 1987. She started to work at a bank during the day and styled hair and nails in the evenings. During this time she also wrote poetry and children's books and drew sketches.

In 1987 Florence decided to continue her athletic career and asked her former coach, Bob Kersee, to help her train for the 1988 Olympic Trials. Her training was hard. She watched a tape of Ben Johnson's 100-meter world's record to improve her start. Florence would use her lunch hours to workout and in the evenings she earned extra money as a part-time beautician and often trained until midnight. Florence left the bank and took a part-time position in the employee relations department with Anheuser-Busch. She also received support and encouragement from her new boyfriend, Al Joyner, who was a triple-jumper and won the 1984 Olympic gold medal. They were later married in Las Vegas, Nevada, in October 1987.

At the 1987 World Championship Games, she was a member of the U.S. gold-medal-winning relay team and won a second place award for the 200-meter event in Rome, Italy. This win encouraged her to improve and try to be the best, so she started daily track and sit-up workouts as well as a weight-lifting program four times a week. Florence contributed her improved performance to a more relaxed running style and concentration on herself.

Shortly after the Olympic Trials Florence fired her former coach and replaced him with her husband, Al Joyner. She made this decision because she needed full time attention and Bob Kersee was coaching six other athletes. Florence contributed her success in running the 100 meters in 10.49 seconds to the coaching given to her by her husband. After the Olympic Trials she moved into a higher earning bracket and commanded $25,000 in appearance, an increase from $1,500 in the past. Florence received offers from film producers, fashion magazines, and other advertising media.

At the XXIV Olympiad in Seoul, Korea, in 1988 Florence Griffith-Joyner won the 200-meter event, setting new world's records in both the semifinals and the final race. Also, she achieved a new record in the 100-meter heat and won the gold in the final event. She also won the gold in the 400-meter relay and won the silver medal in the 1,600-meter relay.

Following these victories in Seoul, Korea, Florence received the Sullivan Award and the *Track and Field News* Athlete of the Year

Award. She was announced as the eighth winner of TAC's highest honor for athletic performance, the Jesse Owens Award, during the Congress's 1988 National Convention Banquet on December 1 in Phoenix.

Florence began coaching her husband, Al Joyner, designing clothing, and continued writing children's books. In August 1992, she began acting on the television soap opera "Santa Barbara." She did not participate in the 1992 Olympics, but may consider training for the 1996 Olympic Games to be held in 1996 in Atlanta, Georgia. In 1993 Florence Griffith-Joyner was appointed co-chair along with Tom McMillan by President Clinton to the President's Council on Physical Fitness and Sports.

Florence and Al have one daughter.

Track and Field

Martha Hudson

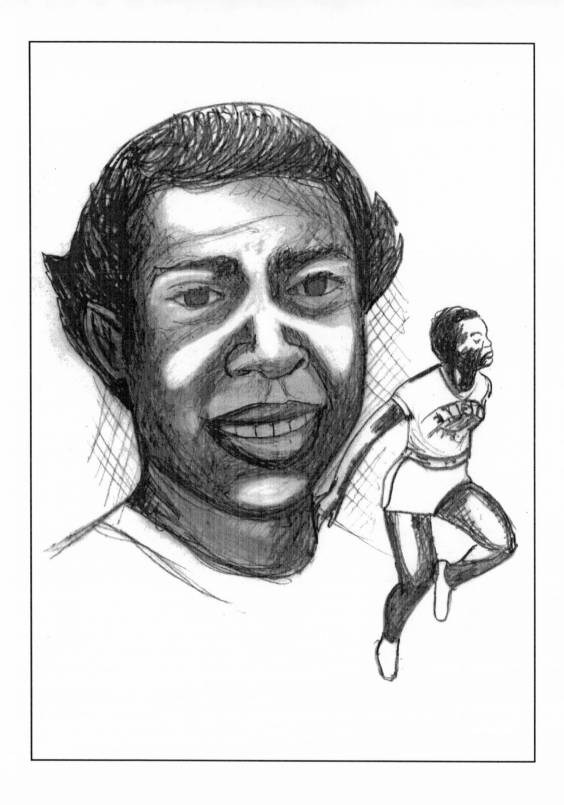

MARTHA HUDSON
(Born 1939—   )

Martha Hudson was recognized as the smallest athlete ever to participate in the Olympics, her height was four feet, ten inches. She was nicknamed "Peewee." In 1960 at the XVII Olympiad in Rome, Italy, Martha ran the first leg on the American 4 x 100-meter relay team that won first place at the Olympics with a time of 44.72 seconds and received a gold medal.

Martha B. Hudson was born on March 21, 1939, in Eastman, Georgia. She was the oldest of three children. Her father worked as a truck driver in a factory in McRae, Georgia, that produced resin, turpentine, and other pine products. Her mother was a housewife.

As a young child Martha liked to compete against the boys in running and most of the time she would outrun them. She attended Twin City High School, where she played basketball and ran track. While in high school she received medals for her outstanding performance in both sports. Martha was invited to attend the summer track and field clinics at Tennessee State University for three summers. Martha was a member of the first group of high school girls to be a part of the program in 1955.

In 1957, Martha graduated as salutatorian from Twin City High School and received a work-aid scholarship to Tennessee State University. While at the university, she participated in national and international competition for six years and in twenty meets. For four years as a student at Tennessee State, she won her letter in track.

In 1959, Martha was the winner of the 100-yard dash in the National AAU Indoor Championships held in Chicago, Illinois.

She was a member of the winning 440-yard medley relay team at the National AAU Indoor Championships in Washington, D.C. She also won the 50-yard dash at that competition. She was a winner of the 60-meter dash at the Tennessee State University in Nashville, Tennessee.

Martha was the holder of the 75-yard dash record in 1959. She was an alternate in the U.S. Pan American Games in Chicago, Illinois. She placed third in the 60-yard dash in the Pan American Games.

Martha was listed by the AAU as the holder of the American girls' championships and noteworthy performance records in the 50- and 75-yard dashes and in the 50- and 75-meter runs. In 1959, she was recognized as the AAU All-American.

In 1960 she was a member of the United States Olympic team in Rome, Italy. Martha was a member of the winning 4 x 100-meter relay team that set a new world's and Olympic record in those Olympic Games.

After the Olympics when Martha returned to her hometown, "Martha Hudson Day" was celebrated in her honor. In 1962 Martha graduated from Tennessee State University. She moved to Thomaston, Georgia, and in 1963 she started teaching elementary school. She also worked as a basketball coach for the elementary school girls.

Track and Field

Barbara Jones

BARBARA JONES
(Born 1937—   )

Barbara Jones won two Olympic gold medals, which made her one of five American women ever to win more than one gold medal. In 1952 and 1960 she was a member of the U.S. 4 x 100-meter relay teams that won gold medals. In 1952 she helped set an Olympic record for the 4 x 100-meter relay with a time of 46.14 seconds. In 1960 the score for the relay was 44.72 seconds.

Barbara Jones was born on March 26, 1937, in Chicago, Illinois. At age fifteen, while still in high school she won her first gold medal at the XV Olympiad in Helsinki, Finland. In 1955 she graduated from St. Elizabeth High School. After graduation she became a student at Marquette University.

In 1956 Barbara tried to make the Olympic team but was not successful and she became very upset. She was advised by Mae Faggs, who made the United States relay team, to transfer to Tennessee State University so she could become a member of their track team. Barbara took Mae's advice and transferred to Tennessee State University. She was awarded a work-aid scholarship and she became a member of the track team.

In 1952 in Chicago, Illinois, Barbara was the holder of the Women's Junior Indoor Championship record in the long jump. In 1958 she was listed among the U.S.A. All-Time Top Ten.

Barbara was the holder of five gold medals in the 100-meter dash in the National AAU Championships in 1952, 1954, 1955, 1958, and 1959. In 1958 and 1959 she was recognized as AAU All-American.

In 1959 in Chicago, Illinois, Barbara set a new Pan American Games record in the 100-meter dash and she also won the

60-meter dash and equaled the games' record in that event. This same year in Nashville, Tennessee, Barbara placed second in the 100-meter dash in the Tennessee State Relays. At the 1959 U.S.S.R. Track and Field Meet in Philadelphia, Pennsylvania, Barbara won the 100-meter dash for the United States.

In 1960 Barbara became a member of the winning 4 x 100-meter relay team that set a new record at Corpus Christi, Texas. This same year at Tennessee State University, she became a member of the winning 440-yard medley team.

In 1960 Barbara had many other accomplishments. She set a new Pan American Games record as a member of the winning 4 x 100-meter relay team in Chicago, Illinois. Barbara won and tied the meet record in the 100-meter dash at the Kansas Olympic Development Track Meet in Empire, Kansas. At the Women's Track and Field Trials at Abilene, Texas, Barbara placed second in the 100-meter dash. At the Olympic Games in Rome, Italy, Barbara was the captain of the winning 4 x 100-meter relay team, which set a new world's and Olympic record.

In 1961 Barbara graduated from Tennessee State University. She married Marcellus Slater and they live in Chicago, Illinois. They are the parents of two daughters. Barbara later became a physical education teacher in the Chicago City Schools.

Track and Field

Jackie Joyner-Kersee

JACKIE JOYNER-KERSEE
(Born 1962—   )

Jackie Joyner-Kersee is the first American athlete to hold the world's multi-event record. She is considered the greatest female athlete in the world, because she won gold medals in 1988 at the Olympics for both the long jump and the heptathlon. At the XXIV Olympiad in 1988 at Seoul, Korea, she set the Olympic and world's records in the heptathlon with 7,291 points and received a gold medal. She also set an Olympic record in the long jump with 24 feet, 3½ inches (7.40 meters) and received a gold medal.

Jackie was born on March 3, 1962, in East St. Louis, Illinois. She was the second of four children born to Alfred and Mary Joyner, who were teenagers when they married. Jackie's grandmother named her after First Lady Jacqueline Kennedy. Jackie's father was a construction worker and moved to different cities to work until he got a job as a railroad switch operator in Springfield, Illinois, about two hours away from their home. Her mother worked as a nurse's assistant. Her mother taught her children to be polite, to be well disciplined, and to be determined to build a better life for themselves.

At age nine, Jackie became interested in track and field when she went to the Mayor Brown Recreation Center to sign up for dance. At first her parents did not want her to participate in track and field, but Jackie insisted and she started to win school contests, so they changed their minds. She inherited her love of sports from her father, who in high school had been a hurdler and a football player.

Jackie ran in her first track competition at age nine. Later she started winning and bringing home prizes, sometimes four or five at a time. At age twelve, she could jump more than seventeen feet, and her brother Al became interested in the sport and later became an Olympic gold medalist in the triple jump.

Jackie's coach at the recreation center inspired her to become an expert in more than one sport, so she may one day be able to participate in the Olympics. Jackie attended Lincoln High School and became a member of the track team. At age fourteen she won the first of four consecutive National Junior Pentathlon Championships. When she was in the eleventh grade she set a state record in the long jump of 20 feet, 7½ inches. As a high school student, Jackie played basketball and volleyball and she became known as one of the finest athletes in the state of Illinois.

In 1980, Jackie graduated from high school in the top ten percent of her class. She received scholarships to the University of California in Los Angeles in both basketball and track. She chose the basketball scholarship and became a forward on the team and chose a major in history and a minor in communications. During the summer of 1980, Jackie competed in the United States Olympic Trials and increased her score in the long jump to 20 feet, 9¾ inches.

During Jackie's freshman year in college, her mother became ill with meningitis and went into a coma. After the life-support system was turned off, she died two hours later at the age of thirty-eight. It was during this time that Jackie became close to an assistant coach at UCLA, Bob Kersee, whose mother had died at an early age. It was this coach who saw her talent in track and field and encouraged her to switch from basketball to track. In 1982 and 1983 Jackie set the collegiate records in the heptaphlon. In 1983 Jackie and her brother Al, a student at Arkansas State University and a triple-jump athlete, were selected for the U.S. Track and Field World Championship in Helsinki, Finland. Jackie suffered a pulled hamstring muscle and could not compete.

In 1984, Jackie and her brother qualified for the track and field teams. Jackie's brother won a gold medal for the triple jump and Jackie won the silver medal in the heptathlon with 6,385 points. In 1985 at the Goodwill Games in Moscow, Soviet Union, she became the first female to break the world's record by 202 points with a score of 7,148 points. Also in 1985, after winning four individual events, she won the WCAA title and she became the seventh fastest American athlete in history. *Ebony* magazine considered her to be the best female athlete in the world.

On January 11, 1986, Jackie married Bob Kersee, her coach. This same year in Houston, at the Olympic Festival, she set her second world's record in the heptathlon, scoring 7,161 points. Also in 1986 Jackie received the Broderick Cup as America's top female collegiate athlete. In 1986 and 1987 she received the Jesse Owens Award. In 1987 Jackie won the Sullivan Award as the nation's outstanding amateur athlete and was named the U.S. Olympic Committee's Sportswoman of the Year. Also in 1987 Jackie became the woman's points-standing winner of the Mobil Grand Prix track and field indoor series. At the Pepsi Invitational track meet, she won the long jump.

In 1988 in Seoul, Korea, at the World Championships and the Pan American Games she was named Amateur Sportswoman of the Year by the Women's Sports Foundation for the heptathlon and long jump competitions. Also in 1988 at the Olympics, Jackie won a gold medal in the heptathlon, setting an Olympic and world's record with 7,291 points. She also won a gold medal in the long jump and set an Olympic record with 24 feet, 3½ inches (7.40 meters).

In 1989 Jackie became the first female to receive *The Sporting News'* Waterford Trophy. In 1992 at the XXV Olympiad in Barcelona, Spain, at the age of thirty, Jackie became the first female to win back-to-back medals in the heptathlon. She won another gold medal.

Jackie plans to compete in the 1996 Olympics in Atlanta, Georgia. With her minor in communications from UCLA, she would someday like to pursue a career in sportscasting.

Track and Field

Mildred McDaniel

MILDRED McDANIEL
(Born 1933—   )

Mildred McDaniel in 1956 became the first American female to set an Olympic and a world's record in the high jump. At the XVI Olympiad in 1956 in Melbourne, Australia, she won a gold medal in the high jump with a score of 5 feet, 9¼ inches (1.76 meters).

Mildred McDaniel was born on November 4, 1933, in Atlanta, Georgia. She was the youngest of three children born to Claude and Victoria McDaniel. Her father was a department store clerk at the Montag Company and her mother was a housewife. Mildred started high jumping at a very early age in her parents' backyard. Her family had a large backyard and the children who lived on the block in her neighborhood used it for a playground. They would put two poles in the ground and put a stick between the poles and jump over it.

Mildred attended David T. Howard High School in Atlanta, Georgia, where she started her career in sports as a basketball player. One day when she was a tenth grade student, she was waiting with some other girls in the school gymnasium before their physical education class began. To pass time, they started throwing a basketball to Mildred and she would shoot the ball in the basket. The gym teacher saw Mildred making the shots and asked her to try out for the team. Mildred did not want to because she didn't think she would like playing basketball. The teacher told the students that she would give any girl who would shoot ten straight foul shots a pair of sneakers the next day and she would be a member of the basketball team. Mildred accomplished this goal, received her sneakers, and became the star player on the team.

Basketball became her favorite sport until the season was over and her gym teacher asked her to try out for the track team. At this time Mildred did not know that jumping was a part of track. While on the track field, Mildred saw a girl trying to jump over a bar but she kept knocking the bar down. Mildred was surprised that the girl could not jump over the bar, so her gym teacher gave her a chance to jump the bar and she did. So Mildred started high jumping, running the hurdles, and broad jumping; and she became a member of the relay team.

Mildred graduated from Howard High School and became a student at Tuskegee Institute and she became involved in track and field activities at the institute. In 1953, she won the AAU Outdoor Championship in the high jump. In 1955 and 1956, Mildred won the high jump title in both the indoor and outdoor nationals, where she became known as the outstanding female jumper in the United States with a record of 6 feet, 6½ inches. In 1955, Mildred won the high jump title at the Pan American Games.

At the Olympic Trials she qualified for a place on the U.S. team with a record of 5 feet, 4 inches. In 1956 at the Olympics, Mildred became the first American female to set a record in the high jump, which remained a world's record for almost two years and an American record until 1967. She received a gold medal with a record of 5 feet, 9¼ inches, and she was the only American female to receive a gold medal at the Olympics that year.

Mildred returned to Tuskegee to finish her studies. In 1959 she won a gold medal in the high jump at the Pan American Games. Mildred married Louis Singleton and became a teacher. She resides in Pasadena, California, with her husband.

Track and Field

Edith McGuire

EDITH McGUIRE
(Born 1944—   )

In 1964 Edith McGuire became the second black woman to win three medals at the same Olympics. At the XVIII Olympiad in Tokyo, Japan, she won a gold medal and set an Olympic record of 23 seconds in the 200-meter dash, won a silver medal in the 100-meter dash with a time of 11.6 seconds, and won a silver medal as a member of the 4 x 100-meter relay team with a time of 43.92 seconds.

Edith Marie McGuire was born on June 3, 1944, in Atlanta, Georgia. She was the youngest of four children born to Clifford and Albertha McGuire. Edith graduated from Rockdale Elementary School and Samuel H. Archer High School in Atlanta, Georgia. In high school she played basketball and track. Edith started running track in the eighth grade at Archer, because she could run faster than the other students in her physical education class. In 1960-61, she was crowned Miss Archer High School. She was an honor student and was named best all-around student in her class. Edith received awards in basketball and track and received a scholarship to Tennessee State University.

In 1961 Edith became a student at Tennessee State University with a major in elementary education. She joined the track team and she was very successful in track during her college years. She was voted AAU All-American in 1961, 1963, 1964, and 1966. During seven years of national and international competition, Edith participated in more than fifty meets and she held world, Olympic, Canadian, AAU American, and AAU championship records in the 200-meter and 220-yard dash.

In 1962 Edith was named All-American in three events. In

103

Stanford, California, in 1962 she won the 100-meter dash and anchored the 400-meter relay team for the United States at the U.S.S.R. Track and Field Meet. The same year in Los Angeles, California, Edith placed second in the 100-meter dash at the National AAU Outdoor Track and Field Championships. Also in Columbus, Ohio, she won the long jump in the Ohio Track and Field Invitational Meet.

In 1963 at Columbus, Ohio, at the National AAU Indoor Track and Field Championships, she won the 100-yard dash and the long jump. The same year at the Mason Dixon Games in Louisville, Kentucky, Edith was a member of the relay team when they set a new indoor record. At the same event she won the 70-yard dash. In San Diego, California, Edith won the 100-meter dash at the AAU All-American Women's Track and Field Championships. In Sao Paulo, Brazil, at the Pan American Games, she won and tied the Games' record in the 100-meter dash.

In 1964 in New York, New York, at the Women's Olympic Track and Field Trials, Edith won the 100-meter dash. In Hanford, California, in 1964 at the National AAU Outdoor Championships, she won the 100-meter dash. At Kingston, Jamaica, she became an American record holder in the 220-yard dash. In Los Angeles, California, at the U.S.S.R. Track and Field Meet, she won the 100-meter dash for the United States. In Nashville, Tennessee, at the Volunteer Games, she won the 100-meter dash. In Kingston, Jamaica, Edith set a new American record when she won the 220-meter dash. At the Olympic Games in Tokyo, Japan, Edith set a new world's and Olympic record and received a gold medal in the 200-meter dash. Also at the Olympic Games she received two silver medals, one in the 100-meter dash and the other as a member of the United States' 4 x 100-meter relay team. After Edith returned from Tokyo, Japan, the mayor of Atlanta proclaimed an Edith McGuire Day and the Atlanta Chamber of Commerce presented her a "Native Daughter" trophy. In Philadelphia, Pennsylvania, as a member of the 440-yard relay team, she helped set a new meet record at the U.S.S.R. Track and Field Meet. Edith placed fourth in the contest for Sportswoman of the World and was one of the finalists for the James E. Sullivan Award, which is

104

given to the most outstanding amateur athlete of the year in the United States.

In Columbus, Ohio, in 1965 at the National AAU Outdoor Championships, in the 220-meter dash Edith set a new meet record. In Moscow, Russia, at the U.S.A.-U.S.S.R. Track and Field Meet, she won the 200-meter dash. She also placed second in the 100-meter dash. At Randals Island, New York, at the Olympic Track and Field Trials she won the 100- and 200-meter dashes. In New York, New York, at the U.S.A.-U.S.S.R. Track and Field Meet at Madison Square Garden, she won the 220-yard dash. In Compton, California, at the Compton Invitational Track and Field Meet, Edith won the 220-yard dash. In Columbus, Ohio, Edith became the holder of the Women's Senior Championship Outdoor record in the 220-yard dash.

In 1966 she became the U.S.A. All-Time Top Ten Indoor Champion in the 220-yard dash and became the Indoor winner of the Charles Diggs Award. In Atlanta, Georgia, at the Southeastern Track and Field Meet, Edith won the 220-yard dash. In Frederick, Maryland, at the National AAU Track and Field Championships, she won the 220-yard dash. In Los Angeles, California, at the U.S.A.-British Track and Field Meet, she came in second place in the 100-meter dash. In Berkeley, California, at the All-American Track and Field Meet, she came in second in the 200-meter dash.

In 1966 Edith graduated from Tennessee State College with a degree in elementary education. For eight years she taught in the Atlanta and the Detroit areas. Edith is featured in Coca-Cola's movie *The Sprinter,* which is used throughout the nation for training women in track and field. In 1975 she was inducted into the Tennessee Sports Hall of Fame.

Presently Edith lives in Oakland, California, with her husband, Charles Duvall. They are owners of three McDonald's franchises in Oakland.

Track and Field

Madeline Manning

MADELINE MANNING
(1948—   )

Madeline Manning in 1968 became the first American woman to win a gold medal in the 800-meter run and was the first American woman to break a time of two minutes in the 800-meter run. At the XIX Olympiad in 1968 at Mexico City, she won a gold medal for the 800-meter run and set an Olympic record of 2:00.9. From 1968 to 1980, Madeline was a member of four Olympic teams and she won a silver medal in 1972 for the 4 x 400-meter relay in 3:25.2.

Madeline Manning was born in Cleveland, Ohio. She grew up in the inner city in a housing project and her parents were divorced. She was raised by her mother, who worked as a domestic, and a stepfather. Her mother had four other children. At age three Madeline developed spinal meningitis and doctors told her mother that Madeline probably would not survive and if she did she would be mentally retarded or would not be normal physically. She was ill for eleven years, but the doctors' predictions turned out to be wrong.

Madeline attended John Hay High School in Cleveland, where she began participating in sports. In junior high school she participated in the President's Physical Fitness Program and was noticed to have some abilities in sports. So she was asked if she wanted to try out for basketball, volleyball, and track. She went out for all three and helped each team win the state championship. Madeline even set a new school record when the track team won the state championship. It was at this competition that she was spotted by Alex Ferenczy, who coached a city team for girls and felt she had championship qualities. Madeline was coached by him for one year before she won her first national championship.

In 1964 at the age of sixteen and in the tenth grade, Madeline started running competitively. In 1965 she won her first national title in the 440-yard dash in the Girls AAU National Championship and was placed on the national team to represent the United States in Russia, Poland, and West Germany. From this time on, she became a member of several national teams from 1965 to 1981. In 1966 in Canada, Madeline set the 880-yard indoor world's record of 2:10.2. In Frederick, Maryland, she was a member of the 880-yard relay team that won in the National AAU Women's Senior Track and Field Championships.

In 1967 she won first place in the Outdoor AAU Championship in the 800 meters with a score of 2:03.6. This same year she set the world's record at the Indoor AAU Track and Field Championship in the 800 meters in Oakland, California, with a score of 2:08.4. Also, she won first place in the Pan American Games with a score of 2:02.3. In Montreal, Canada, she won the 800-meter run in the American Track and Field Meet. In Santa Barbara, California, at the AAU National Women's Track and Field Championship, Madeline won the 400-meter dash and set a new American record. Also in 1967 Madeline was named Athlete of the Year and the holder of the Norman E. Seattel Award for the most outstanding female track athlete in the United States.

In 1968 she set new American and world's records in the 800 meters and won a gold medal at the Olympics with a score of 2:00.9. This same year she won first place in both the Indoor AAU Championship and in the Olympic Trials. She placed second in the Outdoor AAU Championship with a score of 2:07.6. In Compton, California, she won the 880-yard run in the Compton Relays. In Nashville, Tennessee, Madeline won the 400-meter dash in the Olympic Development Meet at Tennessee State University. In 1967, 1968, and 1969 *Track and Field News* ranked Madeline number one in the world.

In 1969 Madeline was named Outstanding College Athlete of America and she was named outstanding athlete in various other meets in 1969, 1975, 1976, 1980, and 1981. Also in 1969 Madeline

110

set a new world's record of 2:02.2 in the Europe versus America Games in Augsburgh, West Germany. And she placed first in the AAU Indoor and Outdoor National 880 Championships. The Negro Business and Professional Women's Club awarded Madeline the Woman of the Year award and she received the Outstanding Woman Award from the Camp Fire Girls, Incorporated, in Nashville, Tennessee.

In 1970 Madeline dropped out of competition. This same year she became a mother to a son and named him John. In 1970 she was named Athlete of the Year.

In 1972 Madeline received a silver medal in the 4 x 400-meter relay with a time of 3:25.2 at the Munich, Germany, games. She was captain of the women's Olympic teams in 1972, 1976, and 1980.

In 1975, Madeline set a new American record of 2:00.5 and was named Outstanding Athlete. In the Russia versus Bulgaria versus U.S. Meet, she set a new American record of 2:00.3 and was named the Outstanding Female Track Athlete of the meet. Madeline was inducted into the U.S. Track and Field Hall of Fame.

In 1976 she won first place in the AAU Outdoor Championship with a time of 2:01.0, but she got hurt during the Indoor Championship. Madeline became the first U.S. woman to break the record by two minutes in the 800-meter dash with a time of 1:59.8 and was named Outstanding Female Athlete. In Maryland at the U.S. versus U.S.S.R. she set a new American record of 1:57.9. Also in 1976 Madeline was inducted into the Greater Cleveland Sports Hall of Fame in Cleveland, Ohio.

In 1979 she placed third at the National TAC Championships. In 1980 Madeline won the Melrose Games and the Indoor National Championship with new meet records in the 800 meters. She won the Outdoor TAC Championship in the 800 meters at 1:58.75 and was named Outstanding Female. She was the winner at the Olympic Trials with a time of 1:58.3. Madeline ran in China's International Games and won the 800 meters in 1:59.8.

In 1980 at age thirty-two, she made the Olympic team but did not compete because of the U.S. boycott. She ran one more race and then retired.

Madeline graduated from Tennessee State University with a degree in sociology. She later attended graduate school at Oral Roberts University in the master of divinity program. In 1982 she was ordained as a minister of the Faith Christian Fellowship International. That same year she founded the Friends Fellowship, Inc., a religious organization that counsels women in the Mabel Bassett Correctional Center in Oklahoma City and the Indiana Women's Prison in Indianapolis. She is a contemporary gospel singer and speaker. She has written a book and recorded an album entitled *Running for Jesus*. She feels she was born to touch the lives of other people. Madeline lives in Tulsa, Oklahoma, with her husband, Roderick J. Mims, and son, John L. Jackson III, from an earlier marriage. Madeline and Roderick also have one daughter, Lana Cherelle.

Track and Field

Margaret Matthews

MARGARET MATTHEWS
(Born 1935—)

Margaret Matthews at the 1956 Olympic Trials set a new American record in the broad jump with a score of 19 feet, 9½ inches. But the pressure of the Olympics was too much for Margaret. She became very tense and did not qualify for the long jump at the XVI Olympiad held in Melbourne, Australia. At the same Olympics, Margaret was a member of the United States 4 x 100-meter relay team that placed third and won a bronze medal. In 1958 Margaret became the first American woman to long jump over 20 feet.

Margaret was born on August 5, 1935, in Griffin, Georgia. Her family later moved to Atlanta, Georgia, where she grew up on Butler Street. Margaret's parents had two daughters and one son. Margaret was the only one to finish high school. Margaret's father was a sickly person who worked as a day laborer in construction, and her mother worked at a laundry.

Margaret was inspired to compete in sports by her gym teacher, Mrs. Marion Armstrong-Perkins (Morgan), who taught her in elementary and junior high school. She was also inspired to play sports because she saw athletics as an opportunity to accomplish more than her family had and as a way to gain an education. Margaret saw other young ladies winning gold medals and she felt that she could reach the same goal. As a student at Howard High School in Atlanta, Georgia, she was an honor student and she was a member of the all-state basketball team. Margaret also held the state records in the 50-, 75-, and 100-yard dashes and in the long jump.

In 1953 Margaret became one of the first girls on her block to graduate from high school. After graduation she attended Bethune-Cookman College, but later left to attend Lewis College in Chicago, Illinois. She later transferred from Lewis College to attend Tennessee State University, where she received an athletic work-aid scholarship and she became a member of the track team. While in college her parents were not able to assist her financially, so she would do ironing, washing, and babysitting to earn pocket money.

In 1954 at Harrisburg, Pennsylvania, Margaret was a member of the 800-meter relay team and her performance was noteworthy. In 1956 in Melbourne, Australia, at the Melbourne Olympic Games, she was a member of the winning 400-meter relay team. Also in 1956 as a member of the U.S. national team in Melbourne, Australia, she won a bronze medal.

In 1957 at the National AAU Women's Outdoor Track and Field Championship in Cleveland, Ohio, Margaret was the winner of the long jump. In 1958 she was the first woman athlete from Tennessee State University to hold a world track and field record. In Akron, Ohio, at the National AAU Indoor Championships, Margaret set a new record in the long jump.

In 1958 Margaret had many successes as an athlete. In Nashville, Tennessee, at the Tennessee State Relays she was the winner of the 100-meter dash. Margaret was a member of the 440-yard relay team in the National Women's Track and Field Championship in Morristown, New Jersey. Also at the same competition, she was the winner of the 100-yard dash. And it was at this competition that Margaret became the first American woman to clear over twenty feet in the long jump and with that, she set a new American record.

In 1958 in Warsaw, Poland, Margaret was a member of the winning 4 x 100-meter relay team. The same year in Athens, Greece, she placed third in the long jump as a member of the U.S. national team. In Budapest, Hungary, Margaret was winner of the long jump as a member of the U.S. national team. In Sidney, Australia, she became the holder of the American and world's records in the 100-yard dash as a member of the U.S. national team.

Margaret was AAU All-American for three years in a row, 1957, 1958, and 1959. In Cleveland, Ohio, at the National AAU Women's Track and Field Meet in 1959, she won the long jump. That same year at the U.S.-U.S.S.R. Track and Field Meet in Philadelphia, Pennsylvania, Margaret won second place in the long jump. She also won second place in the long jump at the Pan American Games in Chicago, Illinois. In 1964 Margaret became co-record holder in Sidney, Australia, on the U.S. national team when she won the 100-yard dash.

Margaret graduated from Tennessee State University and married her campus boyfriend, Jesse Wilburn, who was a running back on the Tennessee State University football team. They moved to Memphis, Tennessee, and Margaret became a teacher at Klondike Elementary School and her husband became a coach at Melrose High School. Margaret and her husband have two sons.

Track and Field

Wilma Rudolph

WILMA RUDOLPH
(Born 1940—Died 1994)

Wilma Rudolph was the first African-American woman to win three gold medals in track at a single Olympics. At the XVII Olympiad in 1960 at Rome, Italy, she won three gold medals. She won the 100-meter run with a time of 11.18 seconds and set an Olympic record. She won the 200-meter run with a time of 24.12 seconds. And with Wilma as an anchor of the 4 x 100-meter relay team, the U.S. team won with a time of 44.72 seconds. Wilma's performance in the Olympics is all the more remarkable because she was unable to walk properly until she was eight years old.

Wilma Rudolph was born on June 23, 1940, in St. Bethlehem, Tennessee, and at a very early age she moved with her family to Clarksville, Tennessee. One of twenty-two children, she was born almost two months early to Eddie and Blanche Rudolph. Before Wilma was born her mother had suffered a fall. At birth Wilma weighted only about four and one-half pounds and for a while it did not appear she would survive. But at an early age, Wilma demonstrated great courage and fortitude, and she was able to overcome both double pneumonia and scarlet fever. The illnesses left her with the use of only her right leg. Wilma's father was a railroad porter and handyman and her mother took in laundry and sewing and worked occasionally as a maid. Her parents were determined that Wilma would live, so her mother would carry her ninety miles to a clinic at Meharry Medical College in Nashville, Tennessee, for treatments and at home her mother and other family members would daily massage Wilma's legs.

In 1947, when Wilma was seven years old, she entered Cobb Elementary School in Clarksville and by the time she was in the

121

th grade she did not have to wear her brace anymore. When she entered Burt High School in Clarksville, she was able to run faster than the other girls her age and basketball became the center of her life. She was recognized as the top athlete in her state. She was also recognized as all-state in basketball—Wilma wanted to follow in the footsteps of her older sister, Yvonne, who played on the school's girls basketball team.

The summer of Wilma's tenth grade, she was invited to attend the track training program at Tennessee State College. When Wilma graduated from high school she received an athletic scholarship to Tennessee State University. She made the track team her freshmen year and she became a sprinter. Wilma's sophomore year, 1960, was the year of the Olympic Trials, but she started to lose races regularly to her teammates. The team doctor discovered that Wilma had a persistent tonsil infection, which had been leaving her weak. After her tonsils were removed, Wilma soon regained her position as the fastest runner on the team.

In 1959 in Cleveland, Ohio, Wilma won the 100-meter dash at the National AAU Track and Field Championships. In Nashville, Tennessee, she won the 100-meter dash in the Tennessee State Relays. In 1959 in Chicago, Illinois, at the Pan American Games, Wilma set a new American record as a member of the winning 400-meter relay team.

In 1960 in Corpus Christi, Texas, Wilma won and set a new American record in the 200 meters, and she won the 100-meter dash. In 1960 in Amsterdam, Holland, she won the 100-meter dash in the U.S.A.-European Tour Track and Field Meet.

In 1960 the Governor of Tennessee presented a personal citation for "Outstanding Olympic Performance" to Wilma for winning three gold medals at the Olympics in Rome. This same year she received many awards and honors for her achievements. The National Publishers Association awarded her the Russwurn Award. *The Nashville Banner* named her the year's "Most Outstanding Athlete." *Sports Magazine* named her "Top Performer" in track and field. The European Sports Writers Association voted her "Most Outstanding Athlete of the Year." She received the Helms World Trophy Award, the Associated Press Award as

Female Athlete of the Year, and *The Los Angeles Times* Award for Women's Track and Field. *Mademoiselle* selected her to receive one of its ten annual awards for Outstanding Achievement among Women. And after the Olympics, her hometown, Clarksville, Tennessee, proclaimed "Wilma Rudolph Day."

In 1961 in Stuttgart, Germany, at the U.S.A.-Germany Track and Field Meet, Wilma won and set a new world's record in the 100-meter dash. In Karlsruhe, Germany, at the U.S.A.-West Germany Track and Field Meet, she won the 100-meter dash again. In Columbus, Ohio, Wilma set a new world's record in the preliminaries. In Louisville, Kentucky, with Wilma as an anchor on the winning team, they set a new meet and world's record for the 440-yard relay team.

In 1961 Wilma received many awards and honors. She received both the Frederick C. Miller Award and the "Babe" Dickerson Zaharis Trophy in 1960 and 1961. She was the Sullivan Award recipient. She was also the first American athlete to have her "Frozen Face of Fame" made into wax and put on display in Madame Tussaud's Celebrated London Museum.

In 1962 in Los Angeles, California, at the National AAU Track and Field Championships, Wilma's team won the 440-yard relay. At that same competition, Wilma won and tied the American preliminaries in the 100-meter dash.

In 1956, 1957, 1959, 1960, 1961, and 1962, Wilma was recognized as the AAU All-American. In 1960–62, she was listed as the "Best in the World" in the 100- and 200-meter dashes. In 1963 she received the Christopher Columbus Award of Geneva.

In 1964, Wilma decided not to participate in the 1964 Olympics and to retire on top. In 1966 in Rome, Italy, she anchored the winning U.S. team in the 400-meter relay in the Olympic Games.

In 1967 in Nashville, Tennessee, Wilma was voted into the Tennessee Sports Hall of Fame and is listed in the All-Time Top Ten in the 100 and 200 meters. In 1977, an autobiographical feature story, *Wilma*, was shown on television.

Wilma married her high school boyfriend, Robert Eldridge. They had four children: Yolanda, born in 1958; Djuanna, born in 1964; Robert, Jr., born in 1965; and Xurry, born in 1971.

In 1973 Wilma was inducted into the Black Sports Hall of Fame, in 1980 she was inducted into the Women's Hall of Fame, and in 1983 she was inducted into the U.S. Olympic Hall of Fame. In 1984, Wilma was one of five sports stars selected by the Women's Sports Foundation as America's Greatest Women Athletes. In 1994, she was inducted into the National Women's Hall of Fame.

Wilma was divorced and before her death she lived in Indianapolis, Indiana, and operated the Wilma Rudolph Foundation, which was a nonprofit organization designed to develop young track and field athletes.

She was a special consultant on minority affairs at DePauw University in Indiana. Wilma's family was not able to be with her when she won three gold medals in the 1960 Olympic Games, so she helped to make sure that other athletes' families didn't suffer the same fate in 1988 by becoming a spokesperson and advisory board member for a trust fund established to pay the expenses for family members of the 560 U.S. Olympic team members to travel to Seoul, Korea.

Wilma died November 12, 1994, of brain cancer at the age of fifty-four.

Track and Field

Gwen Torrence

GWEN TORRENCE
(Born 1965—   )

Gwen Torrence in 1992 won two gold medals and one silver medal at the XXV Olympiad in Barcelona, Spain. She won the 200-meter dash in 21.81 seconds and received a gold medal. Gwen anchored the United States' 4 x 100-meter relay team in 42.11 seconds and received a gold medal. She was also a member of the 4 x 400-meter relay team and received a silver medal.

Gwen Torrence was born on June 12, 1965, in Atlanta, Georgia, with the umbilical cord wrapped around her neck. She spent the first five days of her life in an incubator. Her early years were spent at East Lake Meadows housing project. The youngest of five children, she has two brothers and two sisters. Her mother, Dorothy Torrence, and her father separated when she was three or four years old. Her mother supported the family by working as a nanny and housekeeper. Gwen's father died from a stroke when Gwen was eight years old. Gwen's mother remarried a construction worker. The family later moved to Decatur, Georgia.

In high school, her physical education teacher, Ray Bonner, convinced her to run. But Gwen refused to put on athletic shorts or shoes, because she felt her legs were too skinny. She became known as the girl who could run, for her hairstyles, and for being the best dressed. She did not become serious about school until her junior year, even though she always wanted something good out of life. One day her principal came to her classroom and gave her a corsage for her performance in track. From that time on, she would raise her hands after each race and he would give her a corsage. Gwen became the state champion in track and became a record holder in the 100- and 200-meter dashes.

In 1983 Gwen graduated from Columbia High School and received a scholarship to attend the University of Georgia with a major in early childhood education. She was the first member of her family to attend college. While in college, she met Manley Waller, Jr., a former sprinter. They were later married and they have one son, Manley Mekhail Waller III, whom they call "Little Man." Gwen's husband works in computer systems at a sporting goods store and also works as her coach. The whole family assists Gwen in her goal—her son gets her started by clapping two pieces of wood together. Her mother cares for her son while she is training and prepares the family's meals and does their laundry.

Gwen's immediate goal was to run the best time in the world each year. In 1988 at the XXIV Olympiad in Seoul, Korea, she placed fifth in the 100-meter dash and placed sixth in the 200-meter dash. Also in 1988, Gwen was an NCAA champion in the 100- and 200-meter dashes.

In 1991 at the World Championship Games held in Tokyo, Japan, Gwen became a world-class sprinter and won silver medals in both the 100- and 200-meter dashes. She also set a world's record in the 55-meter dash and then set an American record in the 60-meter dash. Gwen's high school celebrated "Gwen Torrence Day" and she was presented with a proclamation, a dozen red roses, and an 18" x 22" photograph of herself, outfitted in a Columbia High track uniform. The photograph is mounted on the school's Wall of Fame.

In Stuttgart, Germany, Gwen won a bronze medal in the 100-meter dash and a silver medal in the 200-meter dash. She ran the second leg on the 4 x 100-meter relay team, which set an American record of 41.49 seconds to win a silver medal. Gwen anchored the winning 4 x 400-meter relay team, which ran the fourth-fastest time ever in 3 minutes, 16.71 seconds, and she received a gold medal.

In 1992 at the XXV Olympiad in Barcelona, Spain, Gwen caused a controversy at the Olympics when she gave her opinion that some of the athletes participating in the 100-meter dash were taking steroids. She later released a statement saying she regretted her remarks. At this Olympics she placed fourth in the 100-meter dash. Gwen received a gold medal in the 200-meter dash with a time of 21.81 seconds. She was a member of the 4 x 100-meter relay team, which finished second, and received a silver medal. Gwen anchored the 4 x 400-meter relay team to win a gold medal with a score of 42.11 seconds. She was honored in her hometown with a parade and another proclamation.

Gwen continues to compete. She has competed in South Africa, Martinique, Trinidad, and Brazil. In 1995, she won the 100-meter dash in Sweden at the U.S. Olympic Track and Field Trials but was disqualified because she stepped on her own starting line before the race. She plans to compete in the 1996 Olympics to be held in Atlanta, Georgia, and she plans to focus on either the 100- or 400-meter events. In 1997 she would like to retire from competition and possibly have another baby.

Gwen presently lives in Lithonia, Georgia, with her husband and their son. She makes motivational speeches at schools. Her career goal is to go to cosmetology school and open a salon.

Track and Field

Wyomia Tyus

WYOMIA TYUS
(Born 1945—   )

Wyomia Tyus became the first athlete to win the 100-meter run twice in the sprint at the Olympics, and in coming back in 1968 to defend her 1964 title, to set an Olympic record and world's record. She received three gold medals and one silver medal in the U.S. women's track and field competition in the Olympics. In 1964 at the XVIII Olympiad in Tokyo, Japan, Wyomia received a gold medal for the 100-meter run with a score of 11.49 seconds and a silver medal as a member of the 4 x 100-meter relay team with a score of 43.92 seconds. In 1968, at the XIX Olympiad in Mexico City, Mexico, Wyomia set an Olympic record and a world's record in the 100 meter run with a score of 11.08 seconds. Also at this same Olympics she received a gold medal and set an Olympic record and a world's record as a member of the 4 x 100-meter relay team with a score of 42.88 seconds. To show solidarity with her fellow athletes, Wyomia dedicated her gold medals to two African-American athletes, John Carlos and Tommy Smith, who were expelled from the Olympics for raising clenched fists on the victory podium during the award ceremony.

Wyomia Tyus was born on August 29, 1945, in Griffin, Georgia. She was the youngest child and the only daughter born to Willie and Marie Tyus. Her father was a dairy worker and her mother was a laundry worker. Wyomia was fifteen years old when her father died; throughout her life she held onto the inspiration she received from him.

Wyomia started participating in sports at Fairmont High School in Griffin, Georgia, by following her three brothers around. She became a member of the basketball team and the top sprinter at her high school. Track only became important to her when she was invited at age fifteen to attend a summer track and field program at Tennessee State University.

In 1963 Wyomia graduated from high school and received an athletic scholarship to Tennessee State University, where she majored in recreation. In 1963 in Moscow, Russia, she won the 100-meter dash and anchored the winning 4 x 100-meter relay team.

In 1964 Wyomia ranked among the top athletes in the 100-yard dash. That year in Hanford, California, she won and equaled the 100-meter dash record in the National AAU Women's Outdoor Track and Field Championships. In Tokyo, Japan, at the Olympic Games, she won and set the new Olympic and world's records in the 100-meter dash. Also at the same Olympic Games she won a silver medal as a member of the United States' 4 x 100-meter relay team. In Louisville, Kentucky, Wyomia won and set a new world's indoor record and meet record in the 70-yard dash in the Mason Dixon Games. In Los Angeles, California, at the U.S.A.-U.S.S.R. Track and Field Meet, Wyomia placed second in the 100-meter dash. And Griffin, Georgia, her hometown, proclaimed "Wyomia Tyus Day."

In 1965 in Kingston, Jamaica, she won and set a new world's record in the 100-yard dash. In 1965 in Louisville, Kentucky, at the Mason Dixon Games as a member of the winning 440-yard relay team, she helped set a new world's and indoor record.

In 1966 in Los Angeles, California, at the U.S.S.R.-British Commonwealth Track and Field Meet, Wyomia won the 100-meter dash. In Berkeley, California, at the All-American Track and Field Meet, she won the 100-yard dash. In Frederick, Maryland, at the National AAU Outdoor Track and Field Championships, Wyomia won the 100-yard dash. In Daytona, Ohio, at the Ohio AAU Track and Field Meet, she won the 100-yard dash. In Atlanta, Georgia, at the Southeastern Track and Field Meet she won the 100-yard dash. And in Frederick, Maryland, at the National AAU Women's Senior Track and Field Championships, Wyomia was a member of the winning 440-yard relay team when they set a new meet record.

In 1967 in Louisville, Kentucky, at the Mason Dixon Games, she won the 70-yard dash. In Montreal, Canada, at the Europe-America Track and Field Meet, Wyomia won the 100-meter dash. In Winnipeg, Canada, at the Pan American Games, she won and set a new Pan American record in the preliminaries. In Oakland, California, at the National AAU Indoor Track and Field Championships, Wyomia won the 60-yard dash. And in Toronto, Canada, at the Maple Leaf Games, she won the 50-yard dash.

In 1968 in Nashville, Tennessee, at the Olympic Development Meet at Tennessee State University, Wyomia won the 100- and 200-yard dashes. In Quanico, Virginia, at the Quanico Marine Relays, she won the 100-yard dash. In Dayton, Ohio, at the Ohio AAU Track and Field Meet, she won and equaled the world's record in the 100-yard dash, and she won the 220-yard dash. At the Olympic Games in Mexico City, Mexico, Wyomia received a gold medal and set both a new Olympic and a world's record. At these same Olympic Games, she received another gold medal as a member of the 4 x 100-meter relay team, which also set an Olympic and world's record. In 1968, Wyomia was listed on the All-Time World List in the 100 meters.

Wyomia retired from amateur athletics in 1969. She graduated from Tennessee State University with a degree in recreation. She married and moved to Los Angeles, California; gave birth to her daughter, Simone; and begin teaching in a junior high school. In 1974, Wyomia joined the first professional track association and for two years she was undefeated.

Wyomia has been involved in many areas, such as being a public relations specialist and a television commentator for track events. She has worked with the U.S. Olympic Committee and the Black Studies Center at the University of California. She has served as a teacher, she's held clinics, she's been a coach and motivational speaker. And she has served as a U.S. Goodwill Ambassador to Africa.

Wyomia presently lives in Los Angeles, California, with her two children, Simone Simberg and Tyus Tillman.

Track and Field

Martha Watson

MARTHA WATSON
(Born 1946—   )

Martha Watson competed in four consecutive Olympic Games. In 1964 she placed second in the broad jump at the U.S. Olympic Track and Fields Trials, which qualified her for the U.S. Olympic team at the XVIII Olympiad in Tokyo, Japan. In 1968 she competed in the broad jump at the XIX Olympiad in Mexico City, Mexico. In 1972 Martha competed in the broad jump and ran on the 4 x 100-meter relay team at the XX Olympiad in Munich, West Germany. In 1976 she competed in the broad jump and ran on the 4 x 100-meter relay team at the XXI Olympiad in Montreal, Canada.

Martha Watson was born on August 19, 1946, in Long Beach, California. When she competed in 1964 at her first Olympic Games, she had just finished high school. That fall she enrolled at Tennessee State University and became a member of the track team. For almost twenty years she competed in track and field. During this time she was the winner of *The Los Angeles Times* "Achievement Cup," which was given to a female who had distinguished accomplishments in varied fields. She became the guest editorialist of *Sports Woman Magazine.*

In 1966 in Dayton, Ohio, Martha won the Ohio AAU Track and Field Meet in the broad jump. In Louisville, Kentucky, she won and set a new meet record in the broad jump at the Mason Dixon Games. In Frederick, Maryland, at the National AAU Outdoor Track and Field Championships, Martha placed second in the broad jump. In Los Angeles, California, at the U.S.A.-British Commonwealth Track and Field Meet, she again placed second in the broad jump.

In 1967 in Minneapolis, Minnesota, Martha won and set a new Games' record in the broad jump at the Pan American Games Trials. This same year she received her first national title when she jumped 20 feet, 6½ inches to win the Indoor Nationals Championship. In Louisville, Kentucky, at the Mason Dixon Games, she was a member of the 440-meter relay team that placed second.

In 1968 in Mexico City, Mexico, at the Pan American Games, she won the broad jump. In 1967, 1968, and 1969 Martha was recognized as AAU All-American.

In 1969–70 in Knoxville, Tennessee, at the Dogwood Relays, Martha won and set the meet record in the broad jump. In 1970, she became the holder of the American broad jump record and co-holder of the world's record in the 60-meter dash.

In 1972 in Claremont, California, she won the broad jump at the Claremont Relays. In Champaign, Illinois, Martha won and set a new American indoor record in the 60-yard dash. In Durham, North Carolina, at the Martin Luther King Games, she was a member of the winning U.S. national team of the 800-meter relay team. In 1972, 1974, 1975, and 1976, Martha won indoor crowns and bettered the American indoor record in 1970 to 20 feet, 11½ inches. In 1973 she bettered it to 21 feet, 4¾ inches. From 1973 to 1975 she accumulated three consecutive outdoor titles.

In 1973 and 1974 Martha was listed in the World's Top Ten in the broad jump. Also in 1974 she was listed in the U.S.A. All-Time Top Ten in the 60-yard dash.

In 1975 in Mexico City, Mexico, Martha received two medals at the Pan American Games—a silver medal in the broad jump and a gold medal as a member of the 4 x 100-meter relay team. In 1976 she was a member of the United States' 4 x 100-meter relay team at the Olympics in Montreal, Canada.

At the end of the 1980 season, she retired from competition and went to live in Las Vegas, Nevada. Martha, a graduate of Tennessee State University, was inducted into the Hall of Fame in 1987 in Indianapolis, Indiana. She worked as a track coach at California State College.

Track and Field

Willye White

WILLYE WHITE
(Born 1939—   )

Willye White became the only female track and field athlete to represent the United States in five Olympics: in 1956 at the XVI Olympiad in Melbourne, Australia; in 1960 at the XVII Olympiad in Rome, Italy; in 1964 at the XVIII Olympiad in Tokyo, Japan; in 1968 at the XIX Olympiad in Mexico City, Mexico; and in 1972 at the XX Olympiad in Munich, West Germany. In 1965 she became the first person to receive the Pierre de Coubertin International Fair Play Trophy from France.

Willye Bertha White was born in 1939 in Greenwood, Mississippi, and was nicknamed "Red," because of the color of her hair. She was the oldest of five children born to Willie and Johnnie White. Her father was a disabled World War II veteran and she was raised by her maternal grandparents. They instilled in her the value of hard work and this work ethic struck with her throughout her career in sports and her studies in the classroom. As she was growing up, Willie changed the *i* in her first name to *y* to stop being mistaken for a boy.

By age ten Willye realized that she had a unique talent and decided to develop it to its fullest. She also realized that she had to believe in herself and that she could not just be as good as others but she must be better. While in elementary school, her cousin asked her to try out for the track team with her. Willye decided to try out for the varsity track team, which was the high school team, and she outran all of the older girls. She made the team and was able to compete in the area Big A championship meets, which were for all the black high schools in the area. From 1953 to 1956, Willye won the 50-yard dash, the 50-yard hurdles, the 75-yard dash, and the running broad jump, and she anchored the winning 300-yard relay team.

The summer of 1956 Willye was recommended and selected to attend the summer track and field training program at Tennessee State University. She became a member of the team and competed that year at the National AAU Meet in Philadelphia. Willye set a new American record in the broad jump with 18 feet, 6 inches in the girls' division. In the women's division she finished in second place, which qualified her for the Olympic Trials being held in Washington, D.C. At the Trials she placed second, and won herself a place on the Olympic team. In 1956 at the XVI Olympiad in Melbourne, Australia, she won a silver medal in the broad jump and set a new American record of 19 feet, 11¾ inches (6.09 meters).

In 1957 Willye set a new record in the broad jump at the National Outdoor AAU meet in the girls' division. In 1958 in Warsaw, Poland, she set a new American record of 20 feet, 2½ inches; it lasted only two days.

In 1960 Willye left Tennessee State University, because the nursing program had been dropped from the curriculum. She went to Chicago because she was interested in the Mayor Daley Youth Foundation women's track team and in nursing. She did not have a scholarship nor did she have much money, so she went to the Chicago Board of Education School of Nursing and became a practical nurse. She was later hired by the mayor with the Board of Health as a practical nurse and became supervisor of the physical fitness program with the Chicago Department of Health. While a student at Chicago State University, Willye also volunteered as a women's track coach, which made her the world's only college player-coach.

In 1961 Willye was on the U.S. team that toured Europe. During the tour she set a new American record in the broad jump at the U.S.A.-West Germany Track and Field Meet at Karlsruhe, Germany, in the broad jump and became the first female to jump 21 feet, ¼ inch. In Moscow she placed second with a score of 20 feet, 11½ inches. In London she won with a score of 21 feet, ¾ inch in the broad jump. Also in London, Willye led the team to victory in the dual meet with England and she won the 100-yard dash.

144

In Chicago, Willye did not have a coach to concentrate on her training in broad jumping but she continued to compete and was still considered the best female broad jumper in the United States. In 1962 she won the indoor and outdoor broad jump championships and she was also the winner of the 50-yard dash. In 1962 at the Poland-United States dual meet, Willye won the broad jump and she placed second in the Soviet Union-United States Meet. In 1962 in Columbus, Ohio, she won the 100-yard dash in the Ohio Track and Field Invitational Meet. In Los Angeles Willye set a new AAU record at the National AAU Track and Field Championship in the broad jump.

In 1963 in Columbus, Ohio, Willye won the 50-yard dash at the National AAU Indoor Track and Field Championships. In 1963 in San Paulo, Brazil, at the Pan American Games, she set a new Games' record. In Los Angeles, California, at the U.S.A.-U.S.S.R. Track and Field Meet Willye set a new American record.

In 1964 in Hanford, California, Willye was the holder of the Women's Senior Championship Record in the broad jump. At the XVII Olympiad in Tokyo, Japan, she was a member of the U.S. 4 x 100-meter relay team and received a silver medal.

In 1965 at Warsaw, Poland, Willye placed second in the broad jump in the U.S. versus Poland Track and Field Meet. In 1966 she was cited for "Fair Play" by USECO. Also in 1966 Willye was the holder of the American record in the indoor broad jump. In 1968 Willye ended a seven-year marriage.

In 1959, 1963, and 1967, Willye won four medals in the combined Pan American Games. In 1968 she was the winner of the Pierre de Coubertin International Fair Play Award. In 1970 in Knoxville, Tennessee, she became a record holder in the broad jump at the Dogwood Relays.

In 1972 Willye was listed in the top ten in the United States in the broad jump. In 1972 her hometown of Greenwood, Mississippi, proclaimed "Willye White Day." Also in 1972, she was named to the Black Hall of Fame.

Willye graduated from Chicago State University in 1976. She still lives in Chicago, Illinois, and is the Director of Recreation Services, Chicago Parks District.

Track and Field

Lucinda Williams

LUCINDA WILLIAMS
(Born 1937—   )

Lucinda Williams was a member of two U.S. Olympic teams. Her first participation was in 1956 at Melbourne, Australia, and her second Olympics was in 1960 at Rome, Italy. In 1960 Lucinda ran the second leg on the U.S. 4 x 100-meter relay team with a time of 44.72 seconds and she won a gold medal.

Lucinda was born on August 10, 1937, in Savannah, Georgia. Her family later moved to Bloomingdale, Georgia. When Lucinda graduated from high school in 1956, she held the record for the state track championship and was also named the outstanding senior athlete. After graduation from high school, she enrolled at Tennessee State University and became a member of the track team. During her first year in college, Lucinda became a member of the U.S. track and field team after having qualified to run the 200-meter dash in the Olympics to be held in Melbourne, Australia.

In 1956 in Philadelphia, Pennsylvania, Lucinda was a member of the winning 4 x 100-meter relay team in the National AAU Women's Track and Field Championships; they set the AAU Championship record. In 1958 in Athens, Greece, at the U.S.-U.S.S.R. Meet in Moscow, Russia, Lucinda was a member of the winning 4 x 100-meter U.S. national relay team.

In Morristown, New Jersey, at the National AAU Women's Championship, she won and equaled the American record in the 220-yard dash. Also in 1958, Lucinda was inducted into the Greater Savannah Athletic Hall of Fame in Savannah, Georgia. In 1958 and 1959 she was recognized as AAU All-American.

In 1959 Lucinda was captain of the U.S.-U.S.S.R. Track and

Field Meet in Philadelphia, Pennsylvania. She placed second in the 100-meter dash at that meet. She was also the winner of the 200-meter dash and she set a new American record.

In 1959 at the Pan American Games in Chicago, Illinois, Lucinda was the winner of the 100- and 200-meter dashes. There, she set a new Pan American Games' record in the 200-meter dash. She was also a member of the winning 4 x 100-meter relay team at this meet.

In Washington, D.C., in 1959 Lucinda was a member of the winning 440-yard medley relay team at the National AAU Indoor Championships. She also won the 220-yard dash.

In 1960 at the Women's Noteworthy Performance in Chicago, Illinois, Lucinda was a member of the winning 440-medley relay team. And during this year, she was nominated for the Sullivan Award and received third place. In 1963 Lucinda served as team manager of the U.S. women's track and field team that toured Europe.

Lucinda received a master's degree in physical education in 1961. She married and taught physical education in Dayton, Ohio. She has a daughter, Kimberly. In 1974 she became a supervisor of health, physical education, and drivers' education in the Dayton, Ohio, Public Schools. Lucinda was the first woman to hold this position.

She works with the Olympic Committee and the state, midwest, and national organizations of the Alliance for Health, Physical Education, Recreation, and Dance. Lucinda talks to young people about being strong, successful, and committed to using one's God-given abilities and talents in a way that will be rewarding in the long run.

ATHLETIC ORGANIZATIONS

Amateur Athletic Union

The **Amateur Athletic Union (AAU)** was organized in 1888 to preserve amateurism. Before AAU there were hardly any lines that separated the amateur from the professional in track and field athletics. Prior to the AAU's establishment, when an amateur competed in professional games and also wanted to compete for prizes in amateur events, he would change his name or geographical location of his next athletic effort. There were some promoters who would announce substantial prizes to attract the outstanding athletes, but when the game was over the winners would find that the promoter had departed with the prizes. There were other promoters who would advertise a strictly amateur meet and would donate a trophy to the winner in view of the spectators, but later would take the trophy back and give the winner cash instead. As the AAU developed, through its creed it became the most important organization in the advancement of sports throughout the world.

In 1889 the AAU drew up a reorganization plan that called for dividing the United States into districts. The original plans called for an organization of individual clubs. All the clubs in the same district formed an association and each association became a separate unit in the AAU. The plan was so successful that in 1890 the AAU adopted the new plan and now there are forty-eight clubs, colleges, schools, and other athletic groups that are a part of the AAU.

The **Sullivan Award** was named in honored of James E. Sullivan, who became secretary-treasurer of the AAU shortly after the organization was formed. In 1930 the AAU gave a memorial trophy in his honor to the amateur athlete who by performance, example, and good influence did the most to advance the cause of good sportsmanship during the year. The award is not just given to athletes who participate in sport events under the AAU but the selections are made on votes cast by the outstanding sports authorities in a nationwide poll.

The American Association for Health, Physical Education, and Recreation

The American Association for Health, Physical Education, and Recreation was organized in 1885 in Brooklyn, New York, by William G. Anderson of Yale University. The organization was originally known as the Association for the Advancement of Physical Education and later became known as the American Physical Education Association. Between 1930 and 1931, the association was reorganized to give representation on the governing bodies to state and district associations and also to sections representing various interests. In 1937 the association merged with the Department of School Health and Physical Education Association and a year later, the organization took the name of American Association for Health, Physical Education, and Recreation and became a department of the National Education Association (NEA). This association represents directors, supervisors, teachers, and interested individuals. The original goals of the organization are stated in its constitution as follows:

(a) To provide for sound and adequate programs in health education, physical education, and recreation education, based upon the needs, interests, and inherent capacities of the individual for his optimum development.
(b) To provide leadership essential to the continued development and improvement of sound and adequate programs in the three related fields.
(c) To promote sound community relationships leading to adequate support for these programs.
(d) To waken and stimulate an intelligent and comprehensive

interest in health education, physical education, and recreation education.

(e) To assist in research and experimentation and to disseminate accurate information.

(f) To co-ordinate the activities of local, state, district, and national associations for health education, physical education, and recreation education.

(g) To affiliate and co-operate with other associations in improving the profession.

(h) To raise professional standards.

(i) To contribute to the individual's understanding of his role as a democratic citizen in America and in the world at large.

The Health Education Division includes Elementary School Health Education, Secondary School Health Education, College Health Services, Safety Education, Community Health Education, School Lunch Section, and Dental Health Section.

The Physical Education Division includes Elementary School Physical Education, Secondary School Physical Education, and College Physical Education.

The Recreation Division includes Industrial Recreation, Public Recreation, Recreational Therapy, and Voluntary and Youth Serving Agencies.

The General Division includes Aquatics, Athletics—Boys and Men, Girls' and Women's Sports, Camping and Outdoor Education, City and County Directors and Supervisors, Council on Equipment and Supplies, Dance, International Relations, Measurement and Evaluation, Professional Education, Research Council, Student, and Therapeutics.

The association serves through its headquarters staff, publications, field services, conventions, divisions, sections, and communities. The association works in cooperation with local, state, and district associations and with many affiliated and related organizations. It constantly works for the good of the profession—studying conditions and trends, setting standards, making recommendations, developing public support, stimulating performance, and making work a more dignified, more interesting, and more worthwhile profession for all. Membership is open to all who are professionally engaged in health, physical education, and recreation. Other interested persons may become associate members on payment of the regular membership fee.

Division for Girls' and Women's Sports

The **Division for Girls and Women's Sports** was formerly the National Section for Girls' and Women's Sports and was part of the American Association for Health, Physical Education, and Recreation, a department of the National Education Association. Its members are those women associates of the American Association for Health, Physical Education, and Recreation who are interested in sports. The purpose of the organization is to promote a wholesome sports program for all girls and women by:

(1) The stating of guiding principles and standards for the administrator, leader, official, and player;
(2) The publication and interpretation of rules technique charts, articles, and teaching aids;
(3) The stimulation and the evaluation of research in the field of women's sports.

The organization was founded in 1899 with Alice Bertha Foster of Oberlin College as chairman. She was appointed to study the many diverse modifications that had arisen when different groups tried to adapt the game of basketball for girls' use. In 1901 the first book of basketball rules was published. In 1905 the permanent committee organization was formed. It was from this committee that the present-day ideals originated, with the main concern being health, play, and recreation as the primary reason for the existence of the games.

As the range of sports in which girls could participate increased, the organization would appoint committees of experts to give guidance in the development of rules and practices governing these sports. In 1927 the National Section on Women's Athletics was organized with more expansion. In 1930 and 1931 the American Physical Education Association was completely reorganized as the American Association for Health, Physical Education, and Recreation, a department of the National Education Association. More sports were added following this reorganization and the division through its sports guides and the Official Rules Committee, with a subcommittee for each sport, approves, makes, and edits rules for the following sports for women: aquatics, archery, badminton, basketball, bowling, fencing, fieldball, field hockey, golf, lacrosse, outing activities, riding, soccer, softball, speedball, tennis, track and field, volleyball and winter sports. The rules are published in their *Sports Library for Girls and Women* by the American Association for Health, Physical Education, and Recreation. In addition to the sports guides and official committee, the committees and their purposes are as follows:

- Finance—To allocate the budget, subject to the approval of the Division Executive Council; to advise on matters of financial policy.
- Officials' Rating—To provide a list of nationally approved officials for badminton, basketball, softball, swimming, tennis, volleyball, etc.; to standardize and improve officiating by providing opportunities for training.
- Audiovisual Aids—To study the whole field of audiovisual aids; to evaluate available sports films; to guide amateurs in the making of films to survey the market for commercially produced films; to encourage commercial production of films with the guidance of teacher-experts; to prepare or edit scenarios for teaching films; to disseminate information to the field on available sources of guidance, films for rent or for sale, literature, etc.
- Public Relations—To disseminate information about the work of the section among educators and laymen; to secure a place for publication of articles of general interest value in periodicals read by laymen.
- Research—To pursue special studies or to cooperate with other Division for Girls' and Women's Sports groups whose work requires certain original data or evaluation; to supervise the

bibliographical work of the sports subcommittees; to approve test materials submitted to guides.

- Standards—To study the field of sports for girls and women and to draw up statements of standards that should guide program development and guidance; to cooperate with other committees that apply the standards to given aspects of the organization of programs.
- Publications—To encourage writing and publishing of special publications; to receive articles from all Division for Girls' and Women's Sports groups and place these for publication; to approve for publication all Division for Girls' and Women's Sports publications except guides.

The organization endorses sound, wholesome sports programs for girls and women under qualified leadership in schools, colleges, and recreational groups. Sports programs for girls and women are promoted so that the outcomes are in the best interests of the individual and of our American way of life.

(1) Girls and women receive opportunities to participate in a wide variety of sports, individual and teams.

(2) The sports program encourages development of interest and ability in activities that are recreational and carry over into other walks of life.

(3) Sports instruction and participation are made available both to the unskilled player and to the skilled player.

(4) Safeguards are furnished to protect the health and welfare of the players.

(5) The leadership is designed to maintain standards conducive to social and spiritual growth as well as physical safety and well-being.

The new division is committed to do even greater work in the future toward improving the quality of leadership and programs of sports for girls and women.

National Recreation Association

In 1906 a group of citizens recognized that there was no place in many of the cities of the country for the safe, healthy, and happy play of children. They organized the Playground Association and successfully promoted local action to correct this situation. This was the beginning of the National Recreation Association, which is a nonprofit, nonpolitical organization serving the recreation needs of Americans of every race, color, and creed. The organization offers some of the following services:

- Communities are aided and encouraged to develop year-round recreation programs to meet the needs of all the people.
- On-the-spot aid is given by trained district representatives, who visit communities all over the country to give individualized help.
- Standards for adequate recreation space, activities, leadership, and administration are developed and public and private groups are helped to attain these standards.
- The world's largest library on recreation is maintained at the National Recreation Association headquarters and is open to students and other interested persons Monday through Friday from 9 A.M.–5 P.M.
- Books on recreation from more than 125 publishers, many of which are on display at the National Recreation Association, are available through the Association. A "Guide to Books on Recreation" is published for the convenience of interested readers and to aid those who wish to order by mail.
- Up-to-date, comprehensive books and pamphlets on programs, materials, and recreation philosophy are published.
- *Recreation* magazine, devoted to the latest happenings in the field, is published ten times a year.
- A recruitment and placement service is operated to help recreation agencies find needed personnel, to aid professional recreation leaders to find job opportunities, to recruit new workers for the field, and to encourage higher standards of training. An internship program is sponsored in cooperation with recreation agencies all over the country.

BLACK WOMEN
IN THE OLYMPICS

1932

Tidye Pickett   Louise Stokes

1936

Tidye Pickett   Louise Stokes
(eliminated in the
semifinal event)

1948

Alice Coachman   Jean Patton
Mae Faggs   Emma Reed
Nell Jackson   Bernice Robinson
Evelyn Lawler   Mabel Walker
Theresa Manuel   Lillian Young
Audrey Patterson

1952

Mae Faggs   Barbara Jones
Catherine Hardy

1956

Earlene Brown	Mildred McDaniel
Isabelle Daniels	Wilma Rudolph
Mae Faggs	Willye White
Margaret Matthews	Lucinda Williams

1960

Earlene Brown	Neomia Rodgers
Shirley Crowder	Wilma Rudolph
Martha Hudson	Willye White
Barbara Jones	Lucinda Williams

1964

Rosie Bonds	Debbie Thompson
Earlene Brown	Kim Turner
Terrezene Brown	Wyomia Tyus
Edith McGuire	Marilyn White
Eleanor Montgomery	Willye White

1968

Margaret Bailes	Madeline Manning
Doris Brown	Mildrette Netter
Barbara Ferrell	Wyomia Tyus

1972

Iris Davis	Mildrette Netter
Gail Fitzgerald	Mattiline Render
Mable Ferguson	Cheryl Toussaint
Madeline Manning	Martha Watson

1976

Debra Armstrong
Evelyn Ashford
Rosalyn Bryant
Chandra Cheeseborough
Gail Fitzgerald

Shelia Ingram
Pamela Jiles
Debra Sapenter
Martha Watson

1980

The United States boycotted the 1980 Olympics to protest the Soviet Union's invasion of Afghanistan.

1984

Jodi Anderson
Evelyn Ashford
Jeanette Bolden
Valerie Brisco-Hooks
Alice Brown
Judi Brown
Chandra Cheeseborough
Robin Campbell
Diane Dixon
Benita Fitzgerald-Brown
Kim Gallagher

Missy Gerald
Randy Givins
Sheri Howard
Jackie Joyner-Kersee
Lillie Leatherwood
Carol Lewis
LeShon Nedd
Pamela Page
Angela Thacker
Kim Turner

1988

Evelyn Ashford
Alice Brown
Valerie Brisco-Hooks
Diane Dixon
Sheila Echols

Kim Gallagher
Florence Griffith-Joyner
Denean Howard-Hill
Jackie Joyner-Kersee

Gail Devers
Gwen Torrence

Jackie Joyner-Kersee

OLYMPIC SITES

OLYMPIAD	YEAR	SITE
I	1896	Athens, Greece
II	1900	Paris, France
III	1904	St. Louis, Missouri
	1906	Unofficial Games held in Athens
IV	1908	London, England
V	1912	Stockholm, Sweden
VI	1916	Games not held during World War I
VII	1920	Antwerp, Belgium
VIII	1924	Chamonix, France Paris, France
IX	1928	St. Moritz, Switzerland Amsterdam, Netherlands
X	1932	Lake Placid, New York Los Angeles, California
XI	1936	Garmisch Partenkirchen, Germany Berlin
XII	1940	Games not held during World War II
XIII	1944	" " " "
XIV	1948	St. Moritz, Switzerland London, England

XV	1952	Oslo, Norway Helsinki, Finland
XVI	1956	Cortina d'Ampezzo, Italy Melbourne, Australia
XVII	1960	Squaw Valley Rome, Italy
XVIII	1964	Innsbuck, Australia Tokyo, Japan
XIX	1968	Grenoble, France Mexico City, Mexico
XX	1972	Sapporo, Japan Munich, West Germany
XXI	1976	Innsbuck, Australia Montreal, Canada
XXII	1980	Lake Placid, New York Moscow, Soviet Union
XXIII	1984	Sarajevo, Yugoslavia Los Angeles, California
XXIV	1988	Calgary, Canada Seoul, Korea
XXV	1992	Albertville, France Barcelona, Spain
XXVI	1994	Lillehammer, Norway
XXVII	1996	Atlanta, Georgia

GLOSSARY

AMATEUR—A person who takes part in an activity, such as sports, as a pastime and not for financial gain.

ARCHERY—The sport of shooting arrows with a bow.

BADMINTON—An Olympic sport for two or four players in which long-handled rackets are used to hit a shuttlecock over a net stretched across a marked court.

BALANCE BEAM—A thin rail a few feet off the ground that is used in gymnastics. It is made of wood and is about 4 inches wide and 16 feet long. The gymnast jumps, steps, balances, and does somersaults on the beam.

BASKETBALL—A game for two teams. There are five players on each team. A team scores points by throwing the ball through one of the baskets. They also try to prevent the other team from making baskets at the other end of the basketball court.

BOXING—The sport of attack and defense using the fists. Boxers are divided into groups by their weight. Boxers in the lightest group are called mini-flyweights; they weigh less than 108 pounds. Boxers in the heaviest group are called heavyweights; they weigh more than 175 pounds. A boxer can fight only in his own or in a heavier weight group. Each fight is divided into rounds, each round lasts two or three minutes. Usually there are ten rounds in a fight. A boxer can win in three ways; whichever way he does it, he must knock the other boxer down for ten seconds. When one boxer is taking a beating the referee can stop the fight, which is called a technical knockout or a TKO.

CANOE RACES—Races for one or two people in a canoe. Canoers use paddles to move their canoes through the water.

CYCLING—Except for the 1904 games, bicyle races have always been part of the modern Olympics. Some of the races are held on an indoor track called a velodrome. Others are held outdoors on roads. Races are held for both teams and individuals.

DECATHLON—A competition that involves ten events in two days. The first day's events are the 100-meter dash, broad jump, shot put, high jump, and 400-meter run. Those of the second day are the 110-meter high hurdles, discus throw, pole vault, javelin throw, and 1,500-meter run.

DIVING—A competition that involves swimmers jumping off diving boards high above the water. While in the air, they do acrobatic turns and twists. In many ways, diving is like gymnastics—each move must be perfectly timed. Diving competitions are scored by points.

EQUESTRIAN EVENTS—Competitions for riders on horses. The horses must be able to jump, turn, balance, and trot at signals from their riders. Riders can compete as teams or individuals.

FENCING—Fighting with swords. Three kinds of swords are used in the Olympics: the foil, the epee, and the saber. The foil is 32 inches long and has four sides. The epee is heavier than a foil and has a three-sided blade. Both the foil and the epee have a guard on the tip. The saber has a blunt tip but a sharp blade. The fencer scores points by touching the other player with the tip of the sword.

FIELD HOCKEY—A game that is something like soccer; both are played on a large field about the same size as an American football field. The field has a goal at each end. In a soccer, two eleven-person teams try to put the ball into the other team's goal. In field hockey, however, the ball is hit with a stick instead of kicked.

FLOOR EXERCISE—An event in gymnastics in which each gymnast tumbles, jumps, and balances and does somersaults on the balance beam.

HAMMER THROW—A sporting event in which, after spinning the body to gain leverage, the contestant hurls an iron or brass ball attached to a handle chain. The ball weights 14.992 pounds. The total weight of the ball, handle, and chain is 16 pounds and their maximum length is 48 inches.

HANGING RINGS—Similar to the rings used by circus performers. Gymnasts hold the rings with their hands and swing and turn. The rings may be held still or they may swing.

HIGH JUMP—A vertical jump for height over a crossbar set on upright standards. A short run-up precedes the jump.

HURDLES—An event in which runners jump over ten small fences. Low hurdles are 2½ feet high. High hurdles are either 3 or 3½ feet high. In the steeplechase race, the runners must jump over hurdles, low bushes, and pools of water.

JAVELIN THROW—A sport that involves throwing a pointed spear after a long run-up. The javelin is made of metal or solid wood with a metal point. Its total length is 8½ to 9 feet, and its weight at least 1¾ pounds.

JUDO—A Japanese sport in which each judo fighter tries to throw the other to the ground or to get him in a hold.

LONG JUMP—An event in which each person runs a short distance to a takeoff board. The runner then jumps forward as far as he or she can. It is important to fall forward after landing.

MARATHON—A footrace of 42.195 km and is an event included in the modern Olympics.

OLYMPIAD—In ancient Greece this was the four-year interval between the holding of the Olympic Games. Today, this refers to the staging of the modern Olympics.

PARALLEL BARS—Used in gymnastics for swinging and balancing. The two wooden bars are 1 to 2 feet apart and about 5 feet off the floor. In the high bar event, the men swing and balance on a single bar set 8 feet off the floor.

PENTATHLON—A contest, for women only, consisting of five different events: 100-meter hurdles, shot put, high jump, long jump, and 800-meter run. The javelin throw and 200-meter run were added recently to make it the women's heptathlon.

POLE VAULT—An event like the high jump except that the bar is much higher. Each person uses a long pole to boost himself up and over the bar.

PROFESSIONAL—A person who makes a living from activities that are also performed by amateurs.

RACETRACK—A course for runners that is divided into lanes. Each runner starts in his or her own lane. The runners in the outside lanes start farther forward than the runners in the inside lanes. Runners may change lanes if they pass each other.

ROWING RACES—Usually held on rivers and lakes. The rowers sit in narrow boats called shells or sculls. They propel the boats by pulling their oars through the water.

RHYTHMIC GYMNASTICS—An event in which the participant uses hoops, balls, clubs and a long, satin ribbon while performing dance movements to music.

SAILBOAT RACES—Races in which the boat sails with the wind around a course set in the water. Each boat goes as close as it can to markers in the water. If a boat touches one of them, the boat is out of the race.

SHOOTING—An Olympic event that uses pistols and rifles for Olympic shooting. The participants shoot at both still targets and moving objects.

SHOT PUT—An Olympic track and field event. With a thrusting motion, during which the wrist is held rigid, the contestant hurls a 16-pound iron or brass ball. High school athletes use a 12-pound shot, women use an 8.8-pound one.

SIDE HORSE or **POMMEL HORSE**—Similar to the vaulting horse except that it has two handles. It is used in gymnastic events.

SOCCER—In the United States, this game is called football in most other parts of the world. Except for the goalkeeper, the players move the ball with the feet. There are eleven people on each soccer team. They try to kick the ball into the goal defended by the other team. They also try to prevent the other team from kicking the ball into their goal.

STADIUM—A sports arena. In ancient Greece, this included a course for footraces.

SWIMMING RACES—These races are held for both short and long distances. Usually the swimmer must use just one kind of stroke in each race. It may be the crawl, the breaststroke, butterfly stroke, or the backstroke.

SYNCHRONIZED SWIMMING—An event in which groups of swimmers perform dancelike patterns in the water.

TABLE TENNIS—Sometimes called Ping-Pong (a trademark). In many ways it is a miniature game of tennis. The court is a 9-foot-long table with a 6-inch-high net in the middle. Players use paddles to hit a small hollow ball to each other.

TEAM HANDBALL—A combination of soccer, basketball, and field hockey. Each team's seven players use a ball about 6 inches wide. They throw it into goals at either end of the handball court.

TENNIS—A game played by two or four people on a rectangular court. Players use rackets to hit a fuzzy ball over the 3-foot-high net. When a player misses the ball or hits the ball out of the court or into the net, the opponent scores a point.

TRACK AND FIELD—One of the most popular Olympic sports. Track events include all kinds of footraces. They may be short races called sprints or dashes. Or they may be long races that last a mile or more. The races are usually held on an oval racetrack. Field events are for throwing and jumping. They are usually held on a flat field.

TRIPLE JUMP—An event in which the runner first hops, then skips, and then jumps.

VOLLEYBALL—A game for two teams. Six players make up each team. The teams stand on a court divided by a high net. They hit the ball back and forth while trying to keep the ball from hitting the ground on its side. They must not hit the ball out of bounds or into the net.

WATER POLO—A team game played in the water. The seven members of each team try to score points by throwing the ball into the other team's goal. Only one hand can be used to touch and throw the ball at any time.

WEIGHTLIFTING—A sport that tests strength. Each weightlifter must raise a weighted bar above his head. If he raises it first to his chest and then over his head, it is called the "clean and jerk." If the weight is lifted over the head right away it is called a "snatch."

WEIGHT THROW—An event in which following a series of body spins, the contestant hurls an iron or brass ball attached to a grip. The total weight is 35 pounds in outdoor competition and 56 pounds in indoor.

WRESTLING—An ancient sport for two men. Using his hands and his body, each wrestler tries to hold or pin the other to the ground. Wrestlers get points for pinning the other, for keeping the other under control, and for escaping hold.

FURTHER SUGGESTED READING

Arnold, Caroline. *The Olympic Summer Games.* New York: Watts, 1991.

———. *The Olympic Winter Games.* New York: Watts, 1991.

———. *The Summer Olympics.* New York: Watts, 1983.

———. *The Summer Olympics.* New York: Watts, 1988.

———. *The Winter Olympics.* New York: Watts, 1983.

Aaseng, Nathan. *Florence Griffith Joyner: Dazzling Olympian.* Minneapolis: Lerner Publications Co., 1989.

———. *Great Summer Olympic Moments.* Minneapolis: Lerner Publications Co., 1990.

———. *Great Winter Olympic Moments.* Minneapolis: Lerner Publications Co., 1990.

Barry, James P. *The Berlin Olympics, 1936: Black American Athletes Counter Nazi Propaganda.* New York: Watts, 1975.

Chambliss, Daniel F. *Champions: The Making of Olympic Swimmers.* New York: Morrow, 1988.

Coote, James. *A Picture History of the Olympics.* New York: Macmillan, 1972.

Durant, John. *Highlights of the Olympics, From Ancient Times to the Present.* New York: Hastings House, 1977.

Eller, Buddy. *USA and the Olympics.* Atlanta, Ga.: Philmay Enterprises, 1983.

The Eternal Olympics: The Art and History of Sport. New Rochelle, New York: Caratzas, 1979.

Fradin, Dennis B. *Olympics.* Chicago: Children's Press, 1983.

Giller, Norman. *The 1980 Olympics Handbook: A Guide to the Moscow Olympics and a History of the Games.* New York: Holt, Rinehart and Winston, 1980.

Greenberg, Stan. *The Guinness Book of Olympic Facts and Feats.* New York: Distributed by Sterling Publication Co., 1983.

———. *Guinness Book of Olympic Records.* New York: Bantam Books, 1988.

Halberstam, David. *The Amateurs.* New York: Viking Penguin, 1986.

Hart-Davis, Duff. *Hitler's Games: The 1936 Olympics.* New York: Harper and Row, 1986.

Haycock, Kate. *Gymnastics.* New York: Macmillan, 1991.

Hugman, Barry J., and Peter Arnold. *The Olympic Games: Complete Track and Field Results, 1896–1988.* New York: Facts on File, 1988.

Hulme, Derick L. *The Political Olympics: Moscow, Afghanistan, and the 1980 U.S. Boycott.* New York: Greenwood, 1990.

Jacobs, Linda. *Wilma Rudolph: Run for Glory.* St. Paul: EMC Corp., 1975.

Jenner, Bruce. *Guide to the Olympics.* Kansas City: Andrews and McMeel, 1979.

Kaufman, Mervyn D. *Jesse Owens.* New York: Crowell, 1973.

Knill, E. *The Olympics.* Santa Barbara, Calif.: Bellerophon Books, 1991.

Lechenperg, Harald. *Olympic Games, 1960: Squaw Valley.* New York: 1960.

Libby, Bill. *Stars of the Olympics.* Alexandria, Va.: Red Dragon Press, 1975.

Litsky, Frank. *The Winter Olympics.* New York: Watts, 1979.

Lypstyle, Robert. *Assignment: Sports*. New York: Harper and Row, 1970.

MacAloon, John J. *This Great Symbol: Pierre de Coubertin and the Origins of the Modern Olympic Games*. Chicago: University of Chicago Press, 1981.

Mallon, Bill. *The Olympic Record Book*. New York: Garland Pub., 1988.

Mallon, Bill, and Ian Buchanan. *The Quest for Gold: The Encyclopedia of American Olympians*. New York: Human Kinetics, 1984.

Mandell, Richard D. *The First Modern Olympics*. Berkeley, Calif.: University of California Press, 1976.

Merrison, Tim. *Field Athletics*. New York: Macmillan, 1991.

Myers, Earl. *Track and Field*. Creative Educational Soc., 1961.

The Olympic Games in Transition. Edited by Jeffrey O. Segrave and Donald Chu. Champaign, Ill.: Human Kinetics, 1988.

Owens, Jesse. *The Jesse Owens Story*. New York: Putnam, 1970.

Page, James A. *Black Olympian Medalists*. Englewood, Colo.: Libraries Unlimited, 1991.

Reich, Kenneth. *Making It Happen: Peter Usberroth and the 1984 Olympics*. Santa Barbara, Calif.: Capra Press, 1986.

Riordan, James. *Soviet Sport Background to the Olympics*. New York: New York University Press, 1980.

Rudean, Kenneth. *Muhammad Ali*. New York: Crowell, 1976.

Sandelson, Robert. *Swimming and Diving*. New York: Macmillan, 1991.

Schaap, Richard. *An Illustrated History of the Olympics*. New York: Knopf, 1975.

Tales of Gold. Chicago: Contemporary Books, 1987.

Tatlow, Peter. *The Olympics*. New York: Watts, 1988.

Turner, Stephen C. *Great Beginnings: Olympics to Super Bowl to World Series to . . .* New York: Simon and Schuster, 1981.

Wallechinsky, David. *The Complete Book of the Olympics, 1992.* New York: Little, 1991.

Walsh, John Evangelist. *The Summer Olympics.* New York: Watts, 1979.

Weyand, Alexander M. *The Olympic Pageant.* New York: Macmillan, 1952.